Up
and
Running
in 30 Days

THIRD EDITION

A PROVEN PLAN FOR FINANCIAL SUCCESS
IN REAL ESTATE

CARLA CROSS

Dearborn™
Real Estate Education

This publication is designed to provide accurate and authoritative information in regard to the subject matter covered. It is sold with the understanding that the publisher is not engaged in rendering legal, accounting, or other professional service. If legal advice or other expert assistance is required, the services of a competent professional should be sought.

President: Roy Lipner
Vice President of Product Development & Publishing: Evan M. Butterfield
Managing Editor: Kate DeVivo
Associate Development Editor: Leah Strauss
Director of Production: Daniel Frey
Production Editor: Caitlin Ostrow
Production Artist: Virginia Byrne
Creative Director: Lucy Jenkins

Published by Dearborn™ Real Estate Education
30 South Wacker Drive
Chicago, Illinois 60606-7481
(312) 836-4400
www.dearbornRE.com

Printed in the United States of America
07 08 09 10 9 8 7 6 5 4 3 2 1

The Library of Congress has cataloged the second edition as follows:

Cross, Carla.
    Up and running in 30 days : a proven plan for financial success in real estate / by Carla Cross—2nd ed.
      p.cm.
    Includes bibliographical references and index.
    ISBN 0-7931-4485-X
    1. Real estate agents—United States. 2. Real estate business—United States—Marketing. I. Title: Up and running in thirty days. II. Title.
HD278.C76 2001
333.33'068'8—dc21   2001017382

Third edition ISBN-13: 978-1-4277-5809-5
Third edition ISBN-10:   1-4277-5809-3

DEDICATION

Up and Running in 30 Days has been inspired by people from two worlds—the worlds of musical performance and real estate sales.

At four I sat down at the piano to pick out the melody and chords to popular songs. That early love of music led to years of performing on piano and flute in front of thousands of people. It also introduced me to the performance concepts that ensure mastery of skills. For those indelible lessons in performance this book is dedicated to two influential teachers—Stacy Green, University of Oregon piano instructor, and Del Chinburg, my flute teacher in grade school and high school. You'll find in this book references to "perfect practice makes perfect," "precision in following the process," and "improvising after you know the tune." These aphorisms aren't mine. They were taught to me by these master performer-teachers, and I learned them by doing them—the only way we really learn.

I stumbled into the world of real estate sales by chance, simply to help my husband. Although I didn't realize it at the time, the musical performance skills I had perfected as a pianist and flutist were exactly what I needed to hone and master the skills of real estate sales. For believing in my abilities and answering my innumerable questions, I acknowledge my first real estate "boss," Robert Grace, who taught me to "just do it." "Go meet people" was his mantra—so, student that I am, I did just that.

Perfect practice makes perfect. We learn by doing. Mastering something takes dedication, tenacity, and determination over time. These are the lessons my mentors taught me, and these are translated into real estate practice in this book. Thank you for allowing me to pass the lessons of my teachers and mentors on to you.

—Carla Cross

P.S. As I write this third edition, I just reread my dedication. Although it's all true, it may sound to you like mastering performance isn't fun! Not true. There's nothing more exhilarating, more motivating, and more inspiring—plus confidence-building—than doing something well enough that you want to do it again! (That's how you'll feel when you sell your first home.) And that's what I'll help you do as you use this resource.

C O N T E N T S

PREFACE

Up and Running in 30 Days is dedicated to all the agents who have taught me "what works." I have enjoyed helping great salespeople launch their careers to high profitability—quickly. *Up and Running* is organized to help you do the same.

In *Up and Running* you have a personal, detailed, workable business-development plan. It has taken me two decades in real estate sales, management, and training to organize and prioritize this business—so you won't have to.

With *Up and Running* you can start your career today, using the same activities top producers use to create multi-million-dollar careers. Congratulations on choosing to become a dedicated, professional, successful salesperson. Before you know it, you will be serving as a success story for the industry!

ACKNOWLEDGMENTS

Thanks are extended to the following reviewers for their contributions to the third edition of this book: Kerry Jacqués, Keller Williams Charleston/Charleston Trident Association of REALTORS® School; Sandi M. Kellogg, CRS, CRI, Resource Training Director, Coldwell Banker Ellison Realty, Inc.; and Kartik Subramaniam, ADHI Schools, LLC.

INTRODUCTION

Congratulations on purchasing your start-up plan for your real estate business. There are many books published for new agents about starting your business. They give you good advice. But this resource has a different goal. My goal is to provide you what's missing in 98 percent of new agents' arsenal:

A proven, prioritized performance plan to bring you success in 30 days

It's great to learn interesting things. It's helpful to get lots of advice. But if you don't know exactly what to do each day to get a sale, what good is all of that advice?

 Big Idea: Advice is useless without the judgment to prioritize it.

Don't get your hopes up that this book is going to tell you everything you ever wanted to know about selling real estate. First, you don't need to know everything before you talk to a human being! Evidence: there are thousands of real estate agents with licenses right now who know a lot, but don't sell much real estate. I don't want you to become one of them!

 Big Idea: Real estate is a *performance art*, not a *knowledge pursuit*.

Why this start-up business plan is unique. Besides books with lots of advice, there are also activity plans available to you. But, again, this start-up plan is distinctly different from those checklists new agents are given to complete. The specific structure and foundations of this start-up plan have been carefully created based on my decades of experience as a

1. top producing agent (I sold 40 homes my first year);
2. coach to hundreds of new agents who became productive fast; and
3. high-level performing musician and music coach.

■ Five Structural Components Work Together to Get You a Sale

As an agent, you learn that every home must have a firm foundation that is structured against natural disasters of your particular area—flooding, landslides, and so on. (I live in Seattle!) You also learn that some builders are great at building foundations, while others aren't so good. It's the same in a business start-up plan. I've identified the five structural components in a business start-up plan that ensure that you get the best foundation, while protecting you from the pitfalls to which the majority of agents fall prey. Here are these components, and why they are so important to your success.

1. **Get you to top performance fast.** As a top producing agent, I learned how to put together and implement a start-up plan that worked. Then, I proved this plan works for others, as I used it to coach hundreds of new agents to success fast. Many of the new agents I hired and coached achieved top 10 percent status their first year in our company, which consisted of 400 agents, including those who had fifteen years' or more experience.

2. **Provide a top-flight "performance plan."** More than experience and background has gone into crafting your start-up plan. I really learned how to craft a good performance plan as a musician and musical performance coach. (I started teaching piano at age 16, and taught private and group piano and flute lessons in colleges for several years.) To learn to do something, you must have a structure that helps you perform correctly from the start. It must give you your next steps—in the right order. It must challenge you at the right times. It must teach you the principles so you can "go on auto" yourself.

Big Idea: This performance plan is the basis for your career success—forever.

Up and Running *will:*

1. Get you to top performance fast
2. Provide a top-flight "performance plan"
3. Help you consistently get better results
4. Get you a sale in 30 days
5. Protect you from adopting the habits of failure

When a learning experience is badly crafted, you can't perform at a high level. (Think trying to use a computer when too much is thrown at you too fast, or when you don't have a chance to get your hands on that computer quickly enough.) When a learning experience is well crafted, you learn well—and fast. (Think Montessori school or the Suzuki violin method.)

I think I learned these lessons so well, because I saw how badly my piano students performed when I couldn't lay out a well-structured performance plan! I saw the need to create a very clear, precise performance foundation, so those who wanted to learn to play the piano (or sell lots of real estate fast) could accomplish their goals. *Up and Running* integrates these performance principles like no other plan you could find!

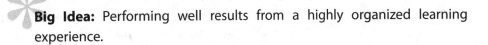

Big Idea: Performing well results from a highly organized learning experience.

3. **Helps you consistently get better results.** As a musician, I know that in order to get great performance fast, I need a way to measure what I'm doing and make adjustments. In music, we listen to our performances, usually with our coach, and evaluate to make adjustments. Then, we play it again with the benefits of our evaluations. That's how we get higher performance. As a real estate coach, that's what I do with my clients: help them look at their performances and make adjustments for higher performance results. So, another big difference in this resource is that I've built in the measurement tools you'll need to analyze your progress and adjust your activities to get the results you want. I haven't just given you activity plans. I've given you the *means to measure your results.* I've given you the analysis tools to make adjustments. I've given you all the tools you need to become a master at *self-management.*

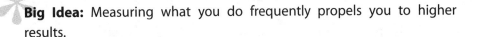

Big Idea: Measuring what you do frequently propels you to higher results.

4. **Get you a sale in 30 days.** When do you expect to make your first sale? If you're like the majority of new agents, you expect to make a sale in your first 30 days in the business. I discovered those expectations when I did a survey of hundreds of agents who had under three months in the business. (The results of that survey are in *Become Tomorrow's Mega-Agent Today!* See the References section.) However, most new agents don't achieve that goal. In fact, about half the new agents who start their careers in any year leave the business that same year! Not only do they not make a sale fast, they don't make enough sales to stay in the business. So, if making a sale your first month is your expectation, you need a start-up plan that gets you into the sales game fast and has you talking with (and working with) many people so that you sell fast (remember, sales is a numbers game).

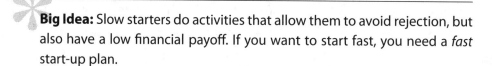

Big Idea: If you want a sale fast, you need a *performance plan* specially constructed to deliver just that.

5. **Protect you from adopting the habits of failure.** As a new agent, at first I honestly didn't know why I was succeeding, but as I began observing the activities of low-producing agents, I noticed they spent most of their time *previewing properties* to "know the inventory." They also spent a significant amount of time in class learning interesting things. They also spent less time on the job (National Association of REALTORS® statistics show successful agents spend many more hours on the job). In contrast, my primary priority was *finding and showing homes to buyers.* I, too, viewed plenty of homes—but took genuine buyers with me to see them. I started contrasting the low-producing agents' plans with mine (although low-producing agents say they have no plan; what they did last week was their plan). My plan was to find and show people homes. Sell as fast as you can! I finally figured out that most new agents avoid the actions that require sales skills. They avoid rejection. They naturally do the activities that are easy: preview homes and sit in class!

Big Idea: Slow starters do activities that allow them to avoid rejection, but also have a low financial payoff. If you want to start fast, you need a *fast* start-up plan.

The School of Hard Knocks

You may read this introduction and say, "Who does she think she is? How come she's giving us all this advice? Did she ever make a mistake?" In truth, my whole first year in the business was one mistake after another. I had no training, no full-time manager, and no mentor. I came from a musical background, not a sales or business background. I had never taken a sales skills course. I didn't attend any type of training school. It was really trial and error, and I'll bet I made every mistake in the book! So, just because I'm writing this book with all this advice, you shouldn't think I was ever perfect—or ever will be.

What I did do was go out into the field and sell a house my first week in the business, and frequently continued doing that while I made all those mistakes. I learned as I went, and I set about doing it better every day. I think my musical and scholastic background helped me stay motivated through that baptism by fire, and caused me to not settle for mediocrity.

The reason I'm writing this book is so you don't have to make the mistakes I made, and here you have a wonderful track to run on.

Big Idea: We learn from our mistakes.

■ What's New in the Third Edition

Up and Running in 30 Days was first published in 1995. Since that time, thousands of new real estate agents have used the program to get "up and running" in 30 days. Now, here's the third edition, which I think is the best yet. Why? Four reasons:

1. I've added information on the **newest trends** and what they mean to you, the new agent, as you start your career, so you can make performance adjustments.
2. I've created a cleaner, **more structured road map** to use this resource to its fullest potential, so you won't get off track. It's also easier for managers to use to coach agents to the plan. For instance, I've added a Technology Budget and Planner so you can integrate technology faster into your business.
3. I've added a section on **scripts and letters** with examples for you to use. I want to make it easy for new agents to get the sales training support needed to make lead generating calls their first week in the business (not everything you need to know, but just enough).
4. I've added many **"Big Ideas"** to ensure that you really grasp and internalize the principles of high performance that so many agents miss, and you get the motivation and inspiration you need to "keep on keeping on."

New trends, lead-generating sources, and skills that are discussed in this edition include:

- The huge trend, the Internet buyer—and how we agents must treat him differently from the traditional buyer
- Information on the trend "paying for leads," and advice on what to pay for and what to stay away from
- Guidance, scripts, and letters to get and follow that Internet lead, a big consideration in lead generation today

New in This Edition

1. Newest trends and what to do about them
2. More structured road map and reporting tools
3. Scripts and letters
4. Big ideas that make training and advice "stand out"

- More technology and marketing resources for you, to support your business
- A sample plan and the format to create your marketing plan to follow up on each of your initial leads

The organization of this new edition has been refined so you can use this resource to its full potential:

- Stronger "get ready" directions for the new agent: information on how to create a budget, how to organize information in three resource manuals, a checklist of "get ready" materials (it's literally your start-up plan, not just a book or an "idea fest")
- Improved clarity in the four-week start-up plan, so you'll know exactly what you are to do
- A detailed, highly structured prioritized system to track your goals and results in each of the four weeks (and great for your manager to use to coach you)
- Explanations of why I've prioritized your sources as "best" to "not so good," so you'll be able to customize your plan to self-manage better and faster
- Built-in "caveats": what to watch for as you start your business so you won't fall into the same failure patterns too many new agents create
- "Big Ideas" to ensure you get the really important concepts of starting and managing your business
- A scripts and letters section (Section 13), where the scripts I introduce in Sections 8 and 9 are detailed so the new agent can learn, use, and refer to them often
- Summaries in each section so you can revisit the crucial points

A challenging real estate market demands focus with a plan. As I write this edition, it is a *shifting market* in most of the United States. It's not nearly as easy to sell real estate as markets shift. In many parts of the United States now, buyers aren't rushing to bid on a home. Sellers aren't anxious, either, to reduce their prices to get a sale. That means you, as a new agent, just can't afford to try to start your career without a great plan! That also means that you must develop a mastery of sales skills to help these more reluctant buyers and sellers make good decisions. The good news: agents that start in more challenging market with a great start-up plan and sales skills do well—forever. Why? They have mastered real estate sales, so they know how to adjust to market changes. They have created their own "insurance" plans. But those who are betting on a fast market to *give* them business will simply be out of business.

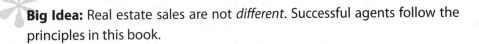

Big Idea: Shifting markets demand a great start-up plan to succeed.

What You *Won't* Find in This Resource

This is not meant as a training manual! Why? Because:

1. I don't want to clutter this start-up plan with lots of ideas on how to do things. As mentioned above, I don't want to distill it to an "idea fest." That's not what you need. A business start-up plan needs to be *separate* from curriculum-based training so the new agent understands the priorities of his business. (Few new agents ever receive or implement a start-up plan, because they're too busy "learning important stuff.") New agents actually think that they can just choose any way to start their businesses, and that they are all the same. Not true. What is true: there are many methods to call on for-sale-by-owners. But if you don't make the sales calls to them, it doesn't matter to your income that you have learned three ways!

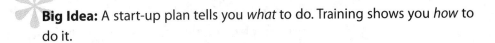

Big Idea: Real estate sales are not *different*. Successful agents follow the principles in this book.

2. New agents need a clear, separate, prioritized, directive plan telling them what to do every day, week, and month to be successful. They need direction from their *first day in the business*. They don't need to do long-term goal-setting. They need to know what to do on Monday—and why.
3. New agents typically can't "see the forest for the trees" and you may receive some bad advice on what you should be doing. After all, most agents don't do lots of business. So, they're going to give you their versions of a "business plan" . . . a very slow business plan! You want to start fast. You just can't use a slow-start business plan.

Big Idea: A start-up plan tells you *what* to do. Training shows you *how* to do it.

But What about the "How"?

It is true that we generally won't start something until we know how to do it. So, in Sections 8, 9, and 10, I've provided a start on "how to"—how to make sales calls and how to execute critical sales skills. You will need to supplement the "how" in your training program. But a new agent doesn't need to know everything about everything to start making sales calls!

References

In the References section, I have provided information to supplement the level of training I'm able to provide you here. There are specific listing tools, selling tools, and sales tools, as well as a training program that is "*Up and Running* on steroids." I've also provided a coaching tool for managers to use with *Up and Running*. Why aren't all these tools included in this book? This resource would be 1,000 pages! Also, each of these tools has specific uses. You wouldn't buy a car that was also an airplane, a boat, and a bike, would you? It would just be too weird! Again, don't let those trees get in your way of seeing the forest (your performance plan).

Are you willing to make an investment in yourself? You have the ability to make hundreds of thousands of dollars a year in real estate. Invest in the coaching and training tools you need now to become that professional you want to be. It amazes me when new agents start their careers and tell me they don't have enough money to invest in the tools they need—or they are unwilling to invest in themselves. Successful professionals always invest in themselves, because they believe in their abilities to attain their goals. What other field could you enter that gives you the ability to earn six figures while you were investing only a few thousand dollars to attain it? (Yes, I said "thousand.") I have never met a successful agent who refused to invest in himself!

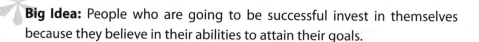

Big Idea: People who are going to be successful invest in themselves because they believe in their abilities to attain their goals.

Learn to Think Like a Top Producer

My long-term goal for you is to teach you how to *think*. I want you to understand the principles in creating a prioritized, successful plan. I want you to implement this plan until you become what some people call an "unconscious competent." Then, no matter the market, you will have the plan and the skills to earn as much money as you want.

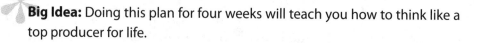

Big Idea: Doing this plan for four weeks will teach you how to think like a top producer for life.

■ **When and How to Use This Program**

When to Start the Plan

Start the plan your first day in the business! Brokers: give this to your new agents during their orientation process. Ask them to read Sections 1–3. Then, meet with the agents to start week one of the start-up plan (see Section 4) within their first week in the business. Why? The new agents expect to make a sale their first month in the business!

Big Idea: Start using this plan your first week in the business.

How This Resource Is Organized

The following table shows a clear idea of how this resource is organized:

How *Up and Running* Is Organized

Overview	Sections 1, 2, 3
Four-Week Plan	Sections 4, 5, 6, 7
Training	Sections 8, 9, 10
Resources	Sections 11, 12, 13
References	Section 14

Overview

Sections 1, 2, and 3. In the first section of this book, we investigate the trends you need to recognize as you start your business. Then, in Section 2, I explain the six principles of a high-producing business. This is a very important section. I want you to know the "why" of your business start-up plan. I'm going to let you in on a secret: this start-up plan isn't just to get you through your first four weeks. It is to set the priorities of your business *forever*. In Section 3, I prepare you to start your plan, explain the manager's role, and give you an overview of your first four weeks. Read these sections right after you finish your orientation with your office so you'll be set to start your week one action plan.

The Four-Week Plan

Sections 4–7. Your actual four-week prioritized start-up plan starts with Section 4, which is your plan for your first week. Section 5 is your plan for week two. Section 6 is your plan for week three, and Section 7 is your plan for week four. This isn't just a book. This is literally *your start-up plan*.

I didn't write this to give you ideas about how to start your business. This is the specific, prioritized, proven action plan for you to dive into and complete each week. This is the action plan your coach will hold you accountable to. This is the action plan that will get you business as fast as you want it! Start your week one action plan in your first week in the business so you'll get a sale fast.

Training: Sales Skills and Marketing Plan

Sections 8–10. In Section 8, I teach you how to contact the four types of lead-generating sources in *Up and Running in 30 Days*. In Section 9, I show you how to create a marketing plan and a promotional tool to stay in touch for as long as it takes. In Section 10, we explore the seven critical sales skills that are extremely important for you to master *right now!* Armed with the sales skills and marketing strategies, along with your lead generating action plan, you are as educated and trained as many agents in their fifth year in the business in these areas. In addition, you know the priorities of a very successful business, and you've been implementing them automatically every week—because this four-week plan is designed using those priorities and principles. You automatically start thinking like a top producer. These are your resources. Remember, they aren't in the four-week plan because I don't want to clutter up your "forest" with too many trees!

Resources: Sample Plan, Measurement Forms, and Scripts, Letters, and Qualifying Forms

Sections 11–13. Here are the *Up and Running* structured forms, scripts, and letters you need to make your plan, implement your plan, and track your plan. I've even included a sample start-up plan for you, along with a sample marketing plan, so you can see how all the pieces of the puzzle fit. These are more training resources for you.

References

Section 14. In the References section, I have listed various support tools that are appropriate for you to use in your first few months in real estate. They include sources for statistics, marketing, Web sites, and software. I've provided information about my training and coaching tools for agents and managers as a further support to you. I realize I can't put everything you need to know in one book, and it wouldn't be organized properly to best train you. (Let's take it one step at a time!) So, when you want to dig deep to create complete systems, when you want to train yourself at a higher level to list and sell, look to those specific resources. To keep the text clean and clear, most of the time I will simply point you to references at the appropriate areas in the text by saying "see the References section."

Symbols to Focus Your Attention

I've added more ways to help you focus on what's important:

1. Big Idea

2. Caution symbol

3. Manager's Tip

You've already seen Big Ideas. I've added that in this edition to draw your attention to major points. You get so much information that I know is very difficult to prioritize. Here's my attempt to help you do so. I've added the caution symbol to provide clarity on the reasons new agents fail. The concepts and skills I'm giving you here aren't just nice to know and do— they're *need* to know and do for you to be successful fast. I've left all the other stuff out! Finally, I've provided tips to managers to use this program, indicated by the manager's tip symbol.

How to Use This Resource

1. **Read the first three chapters as soon as you get the book** in order to get an overview of the principles and structure. If you're a new agent, you'll want to get these chapters read in your first three days in the business. In Section 3, I have a list of "get ready to go" materials. Gather them quickly so you're ready to start your four-week plan. (If you also have the CDs, which are available through Carla Cross Seminars, Inc., *www.carlacross.com,* listen to the CDs that cover these first three chapters, in which I give you personal insights in addition to what's in this resource.)

2. **Start the four-week plan (Sections 4–7).** Remember, since this is literally your start-up plan, you'll want to start the plan your first week in the business. As you proceed in your plan, the week's assignments will refer to the sales skills you'll need to master as you carry out that week's plan. The explanation of the sales skills, marketing plan, and promotional tools are in Sections 8, 9, and 10, and are role-played on your CDs.

■ A Perspective about Training Programs and Start-Up Plans

A new agent doesn't have the perspective to make judgments about the quality of his or her training program or the quality of the start-up plan he or she is given. In fact, most new agents think all training is the same, and that going to the company training program will ensure his success. Neither assumption is true. In addition, new agents think any plan of action given to them by their managers is as good as the next one. That's not true either. In this section, I'll provide you some perspectives about what training can do for you, and what you shouldn't expect it to do. I'll also provide you some ammunition to judge the effectiveness of any start-up plan you're given. As a lifelong performer and coach, I know that the performance models that you're given, and that you follow, predict the kind of performance you give.

The Limitations of Training Programs

I hope your company has a great training program. However, it won't be enough to ensure your success without your implementing your start-up plan for these reasons:

1. Training programs tell or show you the "how." They don't provide a directive performance plan and hold you accountable to it over a period of time so you get your priorities straight. That's coaching, and it must be done by your manager or an outside coach.
2. Most company training programs are focused on the technical aspects of real estate (how to write a purchase and sale agreement, all about financing, and so on).
3. Most training programs do not teach *sales*. Or, if they do, they don't teach sales using the facilitation skills required to ensure you master the sales skills you need to succeed (role-playing countering objections, role-playing giving a listing presentation, etc.) You may conclude that hearing someone tell you how to do a listing presentation, or seeing someone do one, gives you everything you need to make a great presentation yourself. Only role-play, coaching, and performance evaluation will make you a great salesperson.

A Big Training Manual: Does It Equate to Success?

You've finished your training program. You have a huge training manual. Now, what do you do? You know a lot of things, and you have a lot of information in that training manual. But, without *Up and Running,* you still don't know *what do on Monday.* I learned how new agents get the wrong idea about selling real estate firsthand. As a manager, I sent my new agents to the five-day company training program. When my new agents came back, they would ask, "Now, what do I do?" I would get out *Up and Running,* which I had introduced to them in their interview, and remind them that this is a performance plan for *real life.* Sometimes I wished I just had not let them go to training, because they came out of training thinking it was *optional* to start the *Up and Running* plan! Why? They thought information was all they needed to succeed. They didn't have to actually take any actions!

Big Idea: Don't get your priorities wrong because you have been "trained."

Critical Analysis: How Good Is That Start-Up Plan?

You know what your training will do for you. So I hope you are convinced you also need to implement a business start-up plan to put all that information in perspective. But watch out—there are more poor ones than good ones out there. As a CRB (Certified Real Estate Broker) instructor for 12 years, I taught thousands of owners and managers nationally. I saw plenty of poor plans managers shared with me. (These were the plans they were giving their agents, too.) Here are some commonalities of them:

- They are laundry lists of busywork activities interspersed with activities that actually make you money, so the agent doesn't get any evaluative perspective to self-manage.
- They *do not* prioritize lead-generating activities, so the agent thinks all types of lead generation have equal payoffs.
- They *do not* have methods of setting goals, keeping track of results, and analyzing results to make changes quickly. (*Up and Running* provides sales ratios so you learn how many specific actions it takes to get the results you want.)
- They *do* incorrectly prioritize actions. For example, as a high priority, they direct the new agent to "see all the inventory" before doing anything else. The rationale is that it's very important to see all the inventory to build a knowledge base. It is important, but only as it relates to working with buyers and sellers. (It's the means, not the end.) But new agents don't want to do the high-rejection, high-risk activities such as talking to people. So they gladly see all the inventory until it becomes their job descriptions!
- They *do* include plenty of "busywork" as equal priority to lead generating—such as a broker having an agent visit a title company to learn how it operates. This keeps the agent busy and out of the

broker's hair! Also, the new agent loves the broker for a while, because the broker isn't asking the new agent to do those high-rejection activities—those activities that lead to a sale!

Bottom line: No would-be successful agent in his right mind would continue doing this type of plan any longer than he had to, because the successful agent recognizes the plan is a poor one.

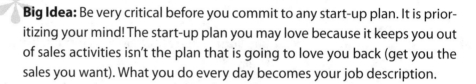

Big Idea: Be very critical before you commit to any start-up plan. It is prioritizing your mind! The start-up plan you may love because it keeps you out of sales activities isn't the plan that is going to love you back (get you the sales you want). What you do every day becomes your job description.

An Effective Start-Up Plan

Here are the six attributes of an effective business start-up plan:

1. Does not give equal weight to all activities
2. Provides an organized activities schedule with certain activities prioritized first because they lead to a sale (in *Up and Running*, these are called "business-producing" activities)
3. Includes an organized activities schedule with certain activities prioritized *second*—and explaining why (In *Up and Running*, these are called "business-supporting" activities)
4. Provides a road map for a continuing plan (remember that "plan for life"?)
5. Builds in the "why" of the plan structure, so you learn to self-manage
6. Has a method to measure and make adjustments in your plan as you progress

Business-Producing Activities Get Highest Priority

Your business actions are either

- Business-producing activities—highest priority
- Business-supporting activities—lower priority

I have to admit that many of the concepts I created in *Up and Running* resulted from my seeing agents fail—again and again. One of the ways they failed was that they couldn't differentiate the value of the activities they would complete in a business day. Because they naturally wanted to avoid rejection, they chose to do the low-rejection activities they felt comfortable completing—which didn't lead them to a sale! So, to help "train their minds," I separated those business activities into two categories:

1. Business-producing
2. Business-supporting

The activities that are highest in priority are those that result in a sale or listing sold. Why? Because those are the only two ways you get a check! These activities are specifically *lead generation, presenting/showing,* and *closing.*

These activities, which top agents call "dollar-productive activities," are listed and performed *first* in your *Up and Running* plan. When I began selling real estate, one of the best agents in the company told me to write at the top of my daily plan, "How will I make money today?" That was good advice. It pays to develop that "success habit" that all top producers have.

Business-Supporting Activities Get Lower Priority

Activities that are not directly lead generating, presenting/showing, or closing are termed *business-supporting activities.* As you may have guessed, low-producing agents complete a variety of business-supporting activities. (They conveniently run out of time before they can spend any time lead generating!) *Up and Running* is structured *not* to let you fall into that bad habit. As you follow the guidelines in *Up and Running,* you will learn to create your daily plan consciously, recognizing the value of your activities.

Big Idea: Schedule and perform business-producing activities first.

Building Success Habits from Day One

The best business-producing plan teaches you to think like a top producer and helps you set the pace for your career. *Up and Running* meets these goals by offering:

- The business-producing plan followed by top agents
- The concepts behind the plan, so you can adapt it to meet your needs
- A specific plan for your first four weeks in real estate, so you can't get off track
- The support and technical activities you should be doing your first four weeks in real estate
- The sales skills and sales calls, including specific scripts, you need to master to complete the business-producing activities in *Up and Running*

Your Most Important "Success" Ingredient: Accountability

You've heard it before. Businesspeople make fancy, multipage, even excellent business plans, and then fail. Why? Because making the plan doesn't ensure success. *Doing* the plan does. (You wouldn't expect that if you studied the life of Mozart you could automatically play a Mozart sonata, would you?)

Big Idea: No success is realized without action.

If action brings about success, then why don't people get into action? Because it's human nature not to! So what is the missing ingredient you need, besides a great start-up plan and action-oriented training so you have the skills to implement the plan? You need someone to be *accountable to.* Study after study shows that we attain our goals when we are accountable, regularly, short-term, to someone. That's because we human beings tend to work on time frames and schedules. (Do you really get your taxes done by April 15 because you love doing them?) Those studies prove we work best on deadlines. We work best when we have a heavy workload. We work best when we have high expectations of ourselves, and we have someone—our coach—who shares those high expectations. (I know all this from being a pianist from age four, and having the privilege of being taught by exceptional piano coaches.)

Big Idea: People succeed not because they have a plan. They succeed because they're accountable to it.

Keeping the priorities straight without a coach is very difficult to do. I know what you're going to tell me. You're goal-oriented. You're a self-starter. You don't need a coach. That's what most new agents say, and over 50 percent of them fail their first year in the business! So, you're better at attaining high performance than Tiger Woods or legendary pianist Horowitz, huh? Hold on a minute. Unless you have already attained high performance in music, sports, and the like, how would you realize that you can't achieve those high levels of performance without a coach?

Big Idea: The habits you form your first month in the business greatly influence your career success—forever.

Most agents have never been in a field that requires such a high degree of self-direction and the mastery of many skills to succeed. So they don't know how easy it will be to get priorities all backwards! They also don't realize how difficult it is to change a bad habit. If you want to be a great pianist, you'd find a great teacher, wouldn't you? So, look at starting your real estate career just like you would look at becoming a great pianist or golfer. You need someone to be accountable to. You need a trained, committed coach, so you have deadlines, expectations, someone to help you keep those priorities straight, and someone cheerleading and believing in you.

Big Idea: No one succeeds alone.

■ Summary: The Full Scope of *Up and Running*

Up and Running in 30 Days offers you a clear, concise start-up plan built on the six foundational structures conceived by me. It provides the "game plan" coaches must have in place to coach you to success. It is also built to *protect you from failure.* It provides you the why, how, how much, and what answers you need to get into action quickly and with confidence.

- **Why.** In *Up and Running* you get the "why." You'll be able to discriminate between effective and ineffective plans and actions long after you're not following the *Up and Running* plan to the letter. You've been given the gift of the tools you need to self-manage your career—forever.
- **How.** In *Up and Running* you get the "how." *Up and Running* explains critical sales skills and sales calls so you can find a partner and practice until you have mastered these skills.
- **How much.** *Up and Running* shows you exactly how to create sales by the numbers, teaching you to measure success and providing reassurance that you are on target.
- **What.** In *Up and Running* you get the "what"—what to do each day.

What's next: read Sections 1–3 so you have the background to start your four-week plan to success. Prepare to start your four-week plan *now,* so you get the habits of success. Here's to a thriving career launch!

The Churning, Shifting Real Estate Industry and What It Means to You

You're launching your career in a rapidly changing market. I've identified nine major trends that are dramatically impacting real estate sales and will, in turn, dramatically impact how you are going to sell real estate. The reason I've included this section is that you are going to go into an office that may have many seasoned agents. These agents are influential. They will speak with authority to you. However, I want you to realize that they are speaking to you from a "historical" perspective (e.g., less than 25 percent of agents have a database or contact management system. That's pretty "historical"—or old school!). Although I want you to respect the seasoned agent's perspective, you are not seasoned. You are launching your career. You may need to do things differently. You will want to launch your business for the future, not the past! In this section, I'll give you advice on how to launch your business so you can take advantage of these trends instead of letting them take advantage of you—or discounting the need to plan with these trends in mind.

 Big Idea: Launch your business for future success.

These nine trends are:

1. Evolving company economic models (various methods of how you'll get paid)
2. Relationship marketing (why it's more important than ever to your career success)
3. Systematizing your business with technology (what you do and don't need to succeed)

1

4. The Internet buyer (how you must prepare to find, work with, and sell to the Internet buyer)
5. Training delivery methods (what type of training works and what is a waste of your time)
6. Coaching (why more agents are seeking coaches, and what you should watch for)
7. Shrinking commissions (what you must do to gain the commissions you want to charge)
8. The Internet-based real estate company (a new player you must recognize)
9. Teaming (is joining a team in your best interest?)

Big Idea: Respect a historical perspective but plan your business to compete for the future.

These trends have permanently affected real estate sales; to be successful in the field you must learn to recognize them—and embrace them in practice. In this section, I've noted the positives in the trend and the "watch out for" aspects of that trend. I'm not endorsing any particular company, concept, or practice. I want to provide you with the critical analysis you need to make your own best decision.

■ Trend One: Evolving Company Economic Models

This first trend addresses how and what you get paid. When I started in real estate over 30 years ago, there was basically one company economic model. Very simply stated, it was this: a person owned a real estate company. We agents worked for that real estate company. For our work, the owner paid us 50 percent of the commissions. It was our one source of revenue from the company. Over these past 30 years, both "variations on that theme" and other types of economic models have emerged from that model. One of the most important decisions you'll make is to decide which model fits you. I'll give you a short description of these models with the pros and cons of each.

The "traditional" split fee model. This model is a variation of the 50/50 commission-splitting model under which I worked. Today, companies using this model generally have a sliding commission split. That is, the more you earn, the more of the total commission you are paid. These plans can get quite complex, so be sure you understand the details of this type of plan.

- **Positives:** Generally, the kind of company that collects relatively more of the commissions offers more service and support to its agents. It has spent many dollars and many years creating a solid company name. For the new agent, these can be very important. To get your money's worth, take full advantage of the company programs, such as training, coaching, and marketing.

- **Watch out for:** Unfortunately, some new agents assume (or are even told) that the company will be responsible for their successes. That's just not true. If it were, then all new agents with a high support company would reach their goals, and no one would fail. What is true is that you, as a new agent, must go out and generate your own leads, no matter the company structure. You may be given some leads from company sources, so you must know what you may be charged for a company lead.

The 100-percent model. About 20 years ago, another economic model emerged in real estate—the "100-percent concept." In this model, agents keep 100 percent of the commissions they earn while paying a "desk fee." This desk fee varies from a few hundred to a few thousand dollars a month, depending on the company. (A variation on this theme is a charge for each transaction. Sometimes a transaction charge is coupled with a desk fee, too.) This model was designed for experienced agents who already know how to run their businesses and don't need many company support services, such as training, coaching, or marketing. Today, many 100-percent companies do not allow the new agent to start at 100 percent because they offer additional training and coaching services to the new agent. These companies have learned that new agents need a high level of support to succeed. From an organizational standpoint, these companies are acting more like the traditional model, while keeping their independent "instincts."

- **Positives:** New agents are drawn to the independent model because they get to keep 100 percent of the commissions. That looks great to the new agent, who is spending a lot more money in the first few months than he or she had budgeted! Having to generate their own leads also forces new agents to be independent, developing the very business habits taught in *Up and Running*.

- **Watch out for:** 100-percent companies assume that an agent has the business skills to run her own business without much support or training. If you're a new agent, that may not apply. Also, there's very little coaching or mentoring in the pure 100-percent model, simply because there is no company dollar to pay for those services.

In addition, check out the other fees you will be paying, because they could add up to about the same as if you were starting in the traditional model company.

The shared revenue model. This model emerged about 15 years ago, paralleling its introduction to business internationally. Here, the company shares additional revenues to commissions, which are usually paid in splits, just like the traditional "split revenue" company. These additional revenues may include profit-sharing, stock options, or company-dollar revenues (what the company gets when an agent sells a home). Generally, these revenues are shared as a reward for helping the company grow. To gain these additional revenues, agents must refer another agent to the company. That way, the company grows, creating more revenue and profit, which are then shared throughout the company with those who helped the company grow.

- **Positives:** Sharing revenues can create a sense of excitement, common focus, and camaraderie. This is motivating to a new agent, who can feel lost in a new business with little day-to-day imposed structure! If the new agent takes full advantage of the training and coaching offered, he can benefit from this environment.
- **Watch out for:** Getting carried away with the excitement! Too many times, agents have been sold on that extra revenue, as if no one had to sell anything to get rich. In addition, you don't just get that extra revenue for showing up. You get it for referring (mini-recruiting) agents to the company. Now you've got two lead-generating jobs: Finding leads for your business and finding leads for your company (recruits). So, find out exactly what those revenues are and how you are going to earn them, before you commit to a shared revenue company. Remember, you still have to start your business by generating your own leads!

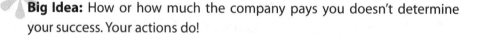 **Big Idea:** How or how much the company pays you doesn't determine your success. Your actions do!

Choosing a Company to Support Your Career Goals

The main question all serious, determined new agents should ask their prospective company is: "How will this particular office, this particular manager, and this particular company help me achieve my career goals?" Too often agents choose a company based on how much of the commission they will be allowed to keep. That's the last item a determined new agent should consider. I proved how faulty that logic was while managing a real estate office. I was competing with an office down the street from me (it was the same company, however). The other office charged the agent a desk fee of $1,000 per month. My office took a percentage of the commissions. The difference to a productive agent was about $10,000 a year (with my office charging that $10,000 more). So, why wouldn't any agent go to that other office? Because they made and kept more money with me. My statistics proved I helped new agents make four times more in their first year than did the less expensive office, where most of the new agents failed—quickly—because they did not receive direction or coaching. In addition, my statistics showed many more of my agents' listings sold, at higher prices and at higher commissions. If you want a successful real estate career, you will choose the company you feel is best suited to support your career goals.

Big Idea: What's important is what you keep, not what you make.

■ Trend Two: Relationship Marketing

Relationship marketing is the key to cutting your expenses and increasing your effectiveness. What is relationship marketing? Creating deep professional bonds with clients over time so that you earn the right to return and referral business. Not only that, it means that you keep in contact with the client forever (see the marketing plan for ideas on how to do that).

In a "fast" market, and without competition, agents used to be able to get away with "order taker attitudes": sell a house, then wait for the next buyer. While great agents didn't operate that way (they practiced relationship marketing), it was still possible to make some money being an "every client is a new one" order taker. Those days are over.

With new competitors who don't try to form relationships and charge lower fees coming into the real estate business, agents who want to charge what I'll call "generous" commissions must switch from a sales mentality to a relationship continuance mentality. Successful real estate demands a firm commitment to your career development; it takes at least three years to build a career, and your clients expect you to commit to their best interests for the long term.

The concepts in *Up and Running* support relationship marketing. You will see that your lead-generating plan, explained in Section 2, begins with your best source of prospects—people you know and meet. Later on, this "best source" becomes your former clients. If you begin with this concept now, you will keep building your best source, as top agents do. I will be referring to the concept of relationship marketing throughout this book.

- **Positives:** As billions of pieces of information and advice clutter the Internet, consumers are looking for trustworthy salespeople. Doing your business as "relationship continuance" differentiates you from these billions of pieces of information, and you can charge the commissions you want to charge.
- **Watch out for:** Assuming that any level of service is enough to charge generous commissions. You've got to work hard to earn that "value-added" reputation.

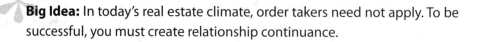

Big Idea: In today's real estate climate, order takers need not apply. To be successful, you must create relationship continuance.

■ Trend Three: Systemizing Your Business with Technology

To be more effective, you need to "duplicate and delegate." The trend today is for agents to move faster and better by systematizing what they do and using technology to do it. The first step is to create checklists and processes for everything you do. These become your systems. For you new agents, take full advantage of every checklist and presentation your company offers. You'll save hundreds of hours of time and energy, because these resources are the result of experts' work.

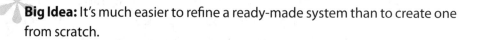

Big Idea: It's much easier to refine a ready-made system than to create one from scratch.

Your second job is to find some technology to support these processes. Your company may have already done that research work for you. It is amazing to me the number of agents who do not take advantage of the technology their company has paid for in research, development, or partnering costs. For example, one large franchise had partnered with a lead follow-up company to ensure that their agents had a simple, effective method to follow their Internet leads. The franchise spent thousands of dollars and hours researching companies to ensure that they chose a company in the agents' best interests. They negotiated a great price for their agents, too. However, only about half of the agents in that franchise took advantage of the thousands upon thousands of dollars their company spent to create that partner agreement. I just can't see any reason not to take advantage of such a great opportunity.

Big Idea: Use the technology and systems your company has invested in for your convenience.

- **Positives:** You're going into the industry as it has matured in its choices for needed technology. It will be easier for you to choose those that are important to your career success.
- **Watch out for:** Invest quickly enough, but don't invest in gimmicks. Also, don't let yourself think that if you have all the technology toys, you'll be successful.

Big Idea: Duplicate and delegate.

From Recipe Box to Software

As a new agent, I was handed a recipe card box and recipe cards and advised to keep all my prospect and client names on those cards. Organizing and tracking contacts with a system is one of those models I've been telling you about. Because my boss directed me to organize and keep track of my contacts, I started that lifelong habit. Although recipe and card files are passé, when you go into your office you probably will still observe some agents trying to keep track of all the names they gather on scraps of paper and in card files—if they keep track of them at all! Why don't they? They haven't gotten into today's world of relationship marketing, or they didn't have a boss like mine, who directed me to start this way. They're still selling "a new client every time."

Big Idea: If every time you sell a home you sell it to a new customer, every year is your first year all over again!

Use technology to support your dynamic business. The easiest way to organize the names of prospects and clients is on a computer. If you're not in the technology world now—jump in. You'll need technology to do the following (these are not my priorities, just a list):

1. Work from wherever you are with a **laptop** so you can find properties, do market analysis, and create presentations anywhere, anytime
2. Organize your prospects, clients, and affiliates (such as mortgage lenders) in a **database** (if you're not extremely computer literate, start with Microsoft Outlook, which almost everyone already has on their computers)
3. Organize your follow-up programs for specific target markets via a **contact management program**
4. Capture and follow up on your Internet leads with **Internet lead follow-up technology** designed for that purpose
5. Measure your **progress to your goals** with specific software
6. Keep in contact with your customers via **cell phone** and pager (you will find it truly amazing how few agents return phone calls)
7. Carry your contacts (database), schedule, and so on with you on a **personal digital assistant**
8. Create a personal **Web site** that promotes you and/or provides your prospects and clients access to information they value, such as updates on their property, marketing, or transaction progress
9. Take pictures with a **digital camera** and add them to your Web site or your flyers
10. Budget for your expenses, track expenses, and create, implement, and analyze your profit and loss statements with **financial software** (such as QuickBooks, Quicken, or Money)

See the References section for resources for these valuable tools.

These include only a few of the technologies agents use in business. Before you buy anything, interview three technology-savvy, high-producing agents in your office and identify the technologies they consider important. Don't expect your real estate company to provide them, although seasoned agents within your organization may be willing to provide direction on the best use of technology. Also, see your manager for advice on the most up-to-date technology you need to perform.

Your Technology Needs

1. A laptop computer
2. Database of prospects, clients, and affiliates
3. Contact management program
4. Internet lead follow-up technology
5. Program to measure your business goals
6. Cell phone
7. PDA or smart phone
8. Personal Web site
9. Digital camera
10. Financial management with software

Your Technology Budget and Planner

Using technology to support your business has become a much higher priority than it was when I wrote the second edition of this book a few years ago. So, I've created a Technology Budget and Planner for you to use to plan your technology acquisitions and implementation. The Planner is in Section 12 and is an assignment for you to complete in your first week in the business. Your assignment will be to decide which technology is most important to you now, and when you're going to purchase and implement it. That way, you can progress in your technology plan every week during *Up and Running*.

Big Idea: Invest in the technology you need NOW, not later.

People want to be sold homes by people, not by computers. Don't hide behind your computer learning new technologies. Don't think you're going to be successful because you know more about e-mail than anyone else. And don't judge start-up plans such as *Up and Running* as less than complete because they don't include details on all the latest technology. What matters is that you stay with the start-up plan, adding your improvisations as you go.

Big Idea: Prioritize it right: Technology provides *support* for relationship marketing.

■ Trend Four: The Internet Buyer

I've added this category since the second edition of *Up and Running in 30 Days* came out in 2001. The number of buyers using the Internet as a homebuying tool has soared from 28 percent in 2000 to 70 percent in 2006, according to the 2006 California Association of REALTORS® survey. The good news is that these Internet buyers are younger and richer than non-Internet buyers. More good news: they rarely look for another agent. They work with the first agent with whom they form a relationship. Shockingly, though, few agents capture these leads effectively. (Agents tell me they take too much time and most inquirers don't buy. Well, what's new? That's sales!)

In order to capture these leads, you need to do the following:

1. Be diligent in answering their inquiries immediately (most agents aren't). This means you need technology to respond to that lead and a system of response.
2. Have a system, supported by technology, to follow up with these people until they "buy or die."
3. Develop communication skills to go from cold Internet inquiry to warm relationship (see Section 9, new in this edition, that addresses exactly how to do that).

■ **Positives:** You're starting in the industry now, so you can follow the recommendations in this resource to enable your business to manage Internet leads.

Capture Internet Leads

1. Answer inquiries immediately
2. Follow up with your leads forever
3. Communicate "warm"

- **Watch out for:** Be wary of taking the advice of well-meaning seasoned agents who may not know the new habits of the Internet buyer, or may not have adjusted their businesses in accordance with them.

Big Idea: Invest in the technology to capture and follow your leads.

Trend Five: Training Delivery Methods

Most new agents are excited to attend their training programs because they think a training program will give them all the information they need to succeed. That's just the tip of the iceberg! A good training program should do much more than that. You should be excited about some types of programs, but not so excited about others. I've included this trend for you so you can choose the type of training that gives you the skills you need to become a pro.

As real estate markets become more challenging, the need for effective training grows. However, money to provide that training shrinks. Some companies have abandoned training altogether. But those who offer training are offering it in two contrasting ways:

1. Some companies provide **action-focused training** in both sales and graduate business areas. That means the skills taught in class are role-played by the students until they master the skills. Often, action plans are assigned, where students put the skills to work in the field.

Big Idea: The more accountable the student, the more he or she learns.

- **Positives:** The student masters skills and gets coaching in skill development and action plans.
- **Watch out for:** The facilitator should be skilled at role-modeling and facilitating, and the student should be held accountable for the activities. New agents: don't sign up for this type of program unless you will do the work to be successful. This is an "on-the-job" high-accountability training program! See the References section for this type of program.

2. Some companies rely on **distance learning** to train agents. In this method, students listen while the lecturer gives information, usually via teleconference or video conference, or sometimes, just video. Sometimes the students can join in discussion. There may be some actions required of the student, but these are generally intellectual exercises, like completing a multiple-choice test. This is obviously not an effective way to learn sales skills! It is a reasonable way to learn facts, although retention is short term (we remember only 10 percent of what we heard three days after we heard it).

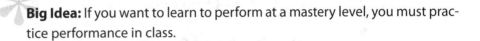

Big Idea: If you want to learn to perform at a mastery level, you must practice performance in class.

If distance learning doesn't provide the best learning experience for the student, why do companies use it? Because it's less expensive, it reaches many students at once, and a manager doesn't have to be personally involved in teaching and holding students accountable.

- **Positives:** The student gets lots of facts fast, and can learn on his own time. It's easy to deliver, because the student just turns on the TV or his computer.
- **Watch out for:** Don't be lulled into thinking you're gaining skills you need to succeed. It's not an effective delivery method to learn skills because there's no practice or accountability.

How to Become a Great Agent—Fastest

Choose a training program that has these two attributes:

1. Student accountability—you'll be expected to perform sales and support activities with a particular level of quality. (Kind of like driving school.)
2. Training program content and instruction methods—Includes interactive exercises, role-play, case study, and action plan methods focusing on sales plans and skills.

Bottom line: Is the company training primarily a recruiting tool, or is it structured to get you a sale fast? Don't waste your time with a program that's just created to recruit you. Your training program should give you the information and practice to be a successful real estate salesperson—fast.

Big Idea: Training is much too important to be only a recruiting tool.

The Next Generation Company Thinks "New Agent Development"

I hate to drop this on you, but you will not be extremely competent after you have finished company training! Why? Because it takes longer than that to master sales skills and refine your processes and systems. It's like learning to play the piano. Just because you can play a folk tune after four lessons doesn't mean you have mastered playing a Beethoven sonata!

I also know a couple of things about *maintaining* performance. As a pianist, the minute I stop practicing, I don't stay at the same performance level. I go backwards. I also know that the real estate industry changes so quickly I must keep getting training and coaching just to stay even!

The New Agent Development System Way of Thinking

I've started working with companies on a holistic approach to agents. Instead of thinking about new agent training or coaching, I want companies to think of you as a "developable salesperson." That means, from your selection to your orientation, training, and coaching, you are constantly helped to get better at what you do. Your company's and your goal is to master sales.

So, rather than thinking you have been "trained," I want you to think of yourself as a "developable commodity." Companies who starting thinking "new agent development" treat you differently.

1. They start with selecting you properly, so you know exactly what is expected of you and how the company will develop you.
2. Right after you're hired, you experience a great orientation process, so you have all the nuts and bolts out of the way.
3. Within that first week, you go into a coaching relationship with me, your manager, implementing *Up and Running,* because you want to get a sale fast.
4. Within the first six weeks, you enter a high-accountability training program to get the in-depth training you need to gain that great competency.

In other words, the company has put a tight, integrated system into place to ensure that you go from "I don't know a thing" to "I feel competent" and "I'm getting predictable sales results."

I predict that this shifting market will force companies into better hiring practices, which will lead to them thinking in terms of new agent development, not just "adding licenses." This paradigm shift is to your great benefit!

 Big Idea: Think of yourself as a "continually developing" commodity.

■ Trend Six: Coaching

Coaching is:

1. Directed
2. Regular
3. One-on-one
4. Planned communication
5. Focused on action

Coaching is *a directed, regular, one-on-one planned communication focused on action* in which the coach

1. directs action following a particular agreed-on game plan (like *Up and Running*), and
2. holds the person coached accountable to that particular agreed-on game plan.

Think of it like a piano or golf lesson. You take a piano lesson because you want to *play the piano.* You play for your teacher and you practice outside class (your action).

Does everyone in real estate sales need a coach? My short answer: yes. But not for the reasons you may think. Often new agents think they need a coach because they must have all the *answers* to succeed. They wrongly consider a coach an "answer man." These agents are correct in that they won't have all the answers—but no agent I have ever known failed from lack of answers. What agents do need to succeed is *direction and focus.* A coach can help an agent with direction—what to do daily, how to implement a plan, how to measure success, and how to stay focused on what's important.

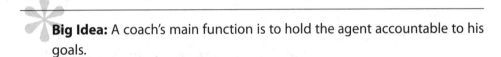

Big Idea: A coach's main function is to hold the agent accountable to his goals.

Big Idea: No one ever failed because he or she didn't *know* enough.

Choosing a Coach

Here are three important points you should consider as you search for a coach:

1. The specific program should be highly organized and precisely outlined with checklists and systems. Ask, "What system are you going to use to coach me?" For example, our Up and Running Small Group Coaching program was organized with a 255-page client manual so the client and the coach know exactly what's going to happen next.
2. The specific program should be related to a "game plan"—a business start-up plan. Ask, "What game plan are you going to use?"

3. The coaches should be trained and coached themselves. Ask, "What's your coaching background, and what sales principles do you believe in?" For example, each of our coaches in the Carla Cross Coaching program has been trained by me and coached regularly by me.

- **Positives:** Having a coach keeps you on track, motivated, and, ideally, inspired to reach your goals.
- **Watch out for:** Your coach is trained and dedicated to your success, and is following a proven game plan (otherwise you'll be paying just to talk to someone every once in a while).

■ Trend Seven: Shrinking Commissions

Commissions are going down, and have been for the past five years. We've just gone through a boom period of real estate, during which hundreds of thousands of new agents entered the business. Although some of them did quite well quickly, they may have not provided the level of customer service the consumer expects. Why? Because they were new. When the market is really great, agents don't have to be too good to make money!

What's different now? In many parts of the country, the market has cooled off. That's actually good for the consumer and good for the agent. Why? Because that means agents have to learn to sell and to provide great customer service to build a business.

Earning a generous commission. Don't just rely on a fast market to get you sales. Build your business with an eye to maintaining and growing it with valued customers. Remember, it costs six to nine times more to get a new customer as it costs to keep an old one. Your job is to find potential buyers, qualify them, sell to them, and then keep in contact with them regularly to show you care more about them than just their money. The consumer was a predictable experience coupled with high trust. They want you to save them time and help them prioritize information. That's what you'll get paid the big bucks for.

In a shifting market, success doesn't come from chance. It comes from implementing the *Up and Running* plan every day.

- **Positives:** A shrinking commission means agents will have to provide true "value-added" service to be paid what they feel they are worth. As a new agent, you can start that way.
- **Watch out for:** Don't settle for cutting commissions because you don't know how you're worth a larger commission. In *Up and Running,* we help you provide dozens of pieces of evidence to buyers and sellers to show them why you're worth the commission you want to charge (and show you, too!).

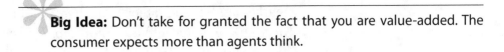

Big Idea: Don't take for granted the fact that you are value-added. The consumer expects more than agents think.

■ Trend Eight: The Internet-Based Real Estate Company

Companies who generate real estate leads via the Internet have been around for years. They've had some challenges getting traction. But now, I believe they've found the formula. They're providing information on their Web sites that is valuable to buyers and sellers, such as market analysis, homes sold, and days on market. They have terrific mapping technologies, which consumers find fascinating. Usually, they charge lower fees than traditional real estate companies and provide fewer services. Sometimes, their agents are salaried.

What this means to you. These Internet companies are providing the kind of statistics that I've urged real estate agents to provide for years. But the magic isn't in spouting statistics. The magic is in interpreting those statistics to your trusting buyer or seller to help them make educated decisions. Remember, your job as a real estate agent today is to help the consumer prioritize information, not just get the information. That was yesterday!

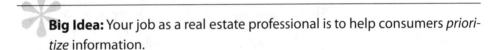

Big Idea: Your job as a real estate professional is to help consumers *prioritize* information.

If you're with an Internet-based real estate company. Your company may charge you for leads. In addition, these companies rightly expect you to follow up on their leads (since they're paying to generate them!). Also, usually they expect you to generate your own leads. So, put to work the *Up and Running* start-up plan, and be absolutely ruthless with yourself in following up on the leads you are given, so both you and your company benefit.

- **Positives:** You can gain leads from the Internet, which can help jump-start your career.
- **Watch out for:** You may get complacent, or think that all you have to do is to sit and snag those Internet leads. Remember that relationship

marketing? Sooner, rather than later, you'll need to turn that writing on your computer into a relationship. *Up and Running* has information on how to do that.

Big Idea: There's no free lunch. Accepting leads doesn't assure your success.

■ Trend Nine: Teaming

What is teaming? It is affiliating yourself with a "rainmaker" agent, an agent who will deliver leads to you, for which you'll pay a portion of your commission. You're teaming up with that agent to do the work that the rainmaker agent doesn't have time to do. First, teaming doesn't mean partnering—two agents working together. If you join a team, *you are working for that rainmaker agent.* Generally, agents who grow teams have been in the business at least a few years. They've developed a large business. To grow their businesses, they need to "duplicate and delegate." So they hire assistants and buyers' agents—agents who work with buyers the rainmaker agent has generated. Many times they hire new agents and train them in their methods.

How Joining a Team Can Help a New Agent

Teaming helps agents obtain leads as they start up business. While agents earn the most in commission dollars when they generate their leads themselves, a new agent may need to pay for someone else's lead generation to begin to develop business. There is a downside to this approach, however. Agents can become complacent and sit and wait for leads. They won't generate—until they get tired of paying for someone else's leads.

- **Positives:** You may be able to jump-start your career with leads given to you.
- **Watch out for:** Be careful to choose a rainmaker who really has enough good leads to distribute to you. Sit in on her team meeting to see how she manages the team. Find out if and how the rainmaker will train you. Find out how much turnover there has been on the team. Find out whether you can sell and list houses outside the team—and how much the rainmaker would charge you if you did. Read the contract the rainmaker asks you to sign and be sure you understand the consequences of your involvement.

Questions to Ask the Rainmaker

1. How many leads will I get per week?
2. How do you manage the team?
3. How will you train me?
4. How much turnover has the team had?
5. Can I sell homes from my own leads, and what will you charge me?

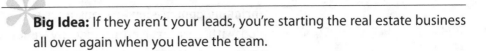

Big Idea: If they aren't your leads, you're starting the real estate business all over again when you leave the team.

■ Summary

The Churning, Changing Real Estate Industry— What It Means to You

The nine major trends discussed here have significance on your business as a new agent:

1. **Evolving company economic models**—No matter which model you choose, the lesson here is that you must generate your own leads to ensure that you create your own real estate business at the income level you desire. Be aware, too, that there is no free lunch. Figure out whether you want the benefits of a specific company structure before you commit.

2. **Relationship marketing**—It's all about the continuance of those leads you're developing. It's no longer a "next" business, it's a "relationship continuance" business. Your job is to generate more leads from those who like working with you by staying in touch—forever.

3. **Systematizing your business with technology**—Too many agents are still doing business "by the seat of their pants." So it's not a business, it's not even a career, it's just a vocation. As a new agent, you must invest in technology to systematize your job so you can do it faster and better.

4. **The Internet buyer**—Now more than three-fourths of buyers are starting with the Internet. New agents must learn how to capture those leads and follow up over a long period of time so that their early efforts at lead generation pay off in the long term.

5. **Training delivery methods**—Choose the kind of training that prepares you to sell lots of real estate fast.

6. **Coaching**—More and more agents are seeking out independent coaches to fill in the gaps left by the constraints most companies and offices face (time, expertise, and money). Most important for new agents is to find a coach who can hold new agents accountable to their business start-up plan. Over 50 percent of new agents don't make it through their first year. Be part of the half that does!

7. **Shrinking commissions**—Consumer demand for better service, coupled with less service provided by generous-commissioned agents, has pushed commissions downward. To earn the commissions they are worth, new agents must get really good really fast.

8. **The Internet-based real estate company**—Companies who offer leads to agents generated from the Internet generally charge lower fees and provide less service to consumers. Generously commissioned agents must not only provide information to consumers, but gain the expertise and trust required to prioritize this information to consumers to help them make informed decisions.

9. **Teaming**—Joining a team within an office is a choice that may be good for the new agent because the new agent will receive leads from the rainmaker, plus high direction and structure. However, there is a high cost for those leads, which must be weighed carefully by the new agent. Not only that, when you're accepting someone else's leads, you're not creating a business for yourself. If your lead source leaves you, you're a new agent again!

With that background, you're ready to learn the six principles of a high-producing business. Armed with the "why" of prioritizing your start-up plan in the manner described in *Up and Running,* we know you'll not only implement this plan correctly, you'll have the invaluable skills to continue these principles throughout your career.

The Six Principles of a High-Producing Business

Too often new agents receive some sort of activity plan from their managers without an explanation of the principles behind the plan—that is, the "why." They just get a list of activities and are told, "Do these things." As soon as they get them done, they think they're off the hook! They don't see that activity plan as a basis for their long-term business habits. *Up and Running* isn't just an activity plan. It's a prioritization of the actions you need to take every day of your whole career life.

 Big Idea: The *Up and Running* concepts are business-planning priorities *for all your career life.*

I'm afraid if you don't know the "why," you may ignore or change some of the parts of my *Up and Running* plan. My friends' child constantly asked, "How come?" (Only it came out of his four-year-old mouth as "How tum?") Even then, he wanted to know why. As an adult, you also deserve to know why each part of this plan has been created. You need the "why" so you can learn to self-manage.

The six principles in the box at the left form the foundation of the "whys"—the recommendations and priorities in *Up and Running*. In this section, I'm also going to give you the other side of the coin: the major reasons new agents fail. I told you I would protect you from failure, and I will! When you see this symbol, you'll recognize when to use caution.

The Six Principles of a High-Producing Business

1. Start the business cycle by talking to people
2. Stay on the business path
3. Prioritize your activities
4. Lead generate like the pros
5. Work the numbers
6. Be accountable to your plan

■ Principle One: Start the Business Cycle by Talking to People

The most important principle in the *Up and Running* business start-up plan is this: your business starts when you start talking to people.

> *". . . the only message that needs to be stressed is to prospect a major portion of your day. Get the scripts and dialogues needed to cold-call, door knock, work expireds and FSBOs. Do the work, and you'll become a great, consistently high-producing agent."*
> —Rick Franz, third-year top-producing agent

To be successful quickly, the most important activity you need to accomplish every day—at least four hours a day—is *to talk to people to get a lead.* This activity starts the business cycle (see Figure 2.1).

The more often you talk to people, the greater your chances to continue the business cycle, to work with and sell someone a property. *Up and Running* will ensure that you spend enough time in the sales cycle to reach your monetary expectations.

Big Idea: The business starts when you start talking to people.

Caution: The biggest reason new agents fail is that they don't contact enough people frequently.

■ Principle Two: Stay on the Business Path

> *"If you don't prospect, the potential for failing in this business greatly increases. I wish I knew how to tell other agents, in a nice way, to get the hell out of my way when they try to discourage me from proactive prospecting!"*
> —Brian Orvis, first-year top-producing agent

Your objective in real estate sales is to get on the *business path* and to stay on it every day until you get to the end of the road—a sale or a listing sold. Figure 2.2 illustrates the business path. It's simply made up of the activities that lead to a sale!

FIGURE 2.1 The Business Cycle

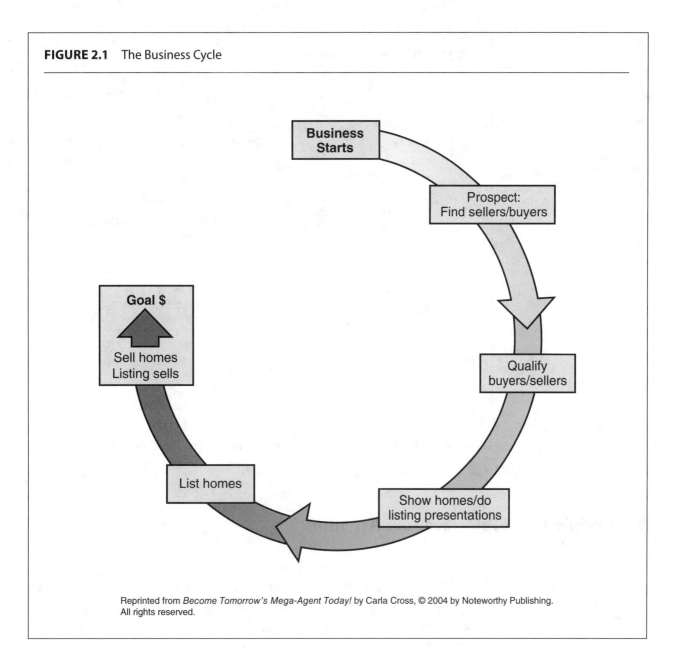

Seems simple, doesn't it? However, many obstacles get in the way—anxiety over making sales calls, fear of not knowing enough, dread of rejection, need for more organization, quest for more knowledge—the list is endless. *Up and Running* will help you stay on the business path, while filling some of those other needs in the correct relationship to your mission—to *sell real estate.*

Caution: New agents fail because they let fear create their "safe" version of their start-up plan.

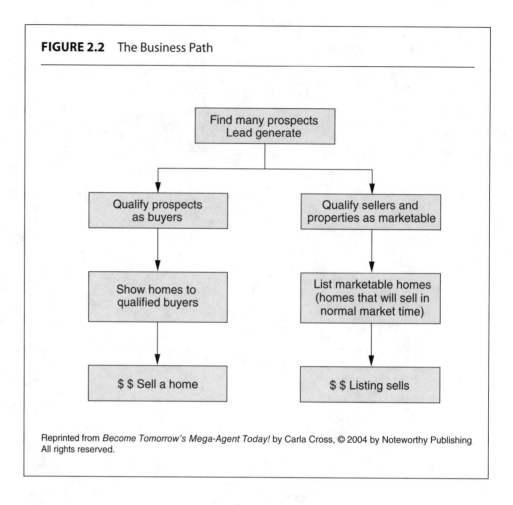

FIGURE 2.2 The Business Path

■ Principle Three: Prioritize Your Activities

"What I would have given to have had a job description indicating a plan of attack. For example, this is how your day must be scheduled: prospecting three hours, follow-up, clerical, etc."
—Rick Franz, now a very successful agent, formerly in hotel management

It's all here, Rick, in *Up and Running*—the hours, the prioritizations, and the concepts behind the schedule. First and foremost, you must spend at least four hours a day starting the sales cycle by lead generating. Where do the other activities fit in? To teach the habits of successful agents, this system has been prioritized for you. As you plan each day, you'll see that your activities fall under two categories:

1. *Business Producing* (activities in the sales cycle)
   - Lead generating
   - Following up on leads
   - Qualifying buyers
   - Showing homes to qualified prospects

- Writing and presenting offers to purchase
- Giving listing presentations to qualified sellers
- Listing marketable properties
- Attending offer presentations on your listings

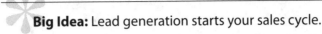

Big Idea: Lead generation starts your sales cycle.

2. *Business Supporting* (activities that support the sales activities)
   - Previewing properties
   - Following up on transactions, making flyers, etc.
   - Sending out mailings (this is not lead generating; it's supporting)
   - Talking to loan officers and title companies
   - Attending meetings
   - Furthering education
   - Creating listing manuals

Big Idea: Learn fast to prioritize your activities as business producing or business supporting.

Caution: New agents who fail think that any activity will get them a sale. (They're the ones in the office "playing computer" or sorting paper all the time.)

This list could be exhaustive. It's common for agents to "hide out" in support activities because they think they are not ready to talk to people. Watch out. This is a sign of creating the *wrong* activities in the business plan. These agents could end up becoming their own assistants—or someone else's!

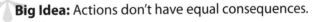

Big Idea: Actions don't have equal consequences.

How Should You Allocate Your Time?

This resources in *Up and Running* are arranged to help you keep these activities in the right priorities. I want to "train your brain" so you can prioritize for yourself long after you've passed your first few years in the business. Figure 2.3 illustrates a prototype schedule that shows how much time you should be spending on each category. Use this schedule to check against the actual plan you design each week. Also, on your weekly schedule, which you will start creating yourself in your week one plan, I have put a reminder of how many hours you should be spending on each category of activities. That way, you can check the "ideal" with your "real" each week. It's another time management tool to help you create the kind of time management habits you will carry with you throughout your career.

Big Idea: Lead generate in the morning as much as possible; you are fresh and there's no competition, because the other agents are still in bed! And remember: the plan you use predicts the results you get.

■ Principle Four: Lead Generate Like the Pros

One of the foundations of *Up and Running* is the *30 Days to Dollars* prioritized lead-generating plan. This plan is built on the solid prospecting principles that make real estate superstars successful. It uses the same target markets (sources of business) and numbers that superstars rely on to build a professional career. To create a high-number, highly profitable career, superstars do the following:

- Secure at least 50 percent of their business from people they know (called *referrals*)
- Gain business by promoting themselves on their successes
- Create a lead-generating plan that meets their monetary goals
- Secure the majority of their business through proactive lead generation (they find people—they don't wait for people to come to them)

Big Idea: (1) The *30 Days to Dollars* prioritized lead-generating plan is your sales-generating goldmine map. (2) Producers spend much more time each day lead generating than do non-producers.

Caution: A heads-up for a shifting market: new agents fail in a market that demands they proactively find leads. Waiting for buyers or sellers to "turn themselves in" in a challenging market is inviting failure.

FIGURE 2.3   Prototype Weekly Schedule

Time Commitments: How to allocate your time to ensure quick success.

Activity	Daily	No./Week	Hours
Lead generate	4 hours	5 days	20 minimum
Open house		Once a week	3–4
Floor time (if scheduled)		1 day	3
Business meeting	1 hour	Once a week	1
Office education	1 hour	1 day	1
Manager/agent coaching		Once a week	½
Previewing homes	2 hours*	5 days*	10

(*first month only)

Schedule

Mon.	8:00 – 8:45	Meet with manager
		Paperwork/calls
	8:45 – 9:30	Business meeting
	9:30 – 12:30	New office listing tour
	Lunch	
	1:30 – 5:30	Lead generate

Tues.   Day off—take it!!

Wed.	8:00 – 9:00	Paperwork
	9:00 – 10:00	Lead generate
	10:00 – 12:00	Previewing
	1:00 – 5:00	Lead generate

Thurs.	8:00 – 9:00	Paperwork
	9:00 – 11:00	Previewing
	12:00 – 3:00	Floor time/buyer tour
	3:00 – 6:00	Lead generate

Fri.	8:00 – 8:45	Paperwork
	8:45 – 9:15	Office class
	9:30 – 12:00	Previewing
	1:00 – 5:00	Lead generate
	7:00 – 8:00	Listing presentation

Sat.	9:00 – 12:00	Lead generate
	1:00 – 4:00	Listing presentation/buyer tour
	4:00 – 5:00	Paperwork

Sun.	12:00 – 2:00	Lead generate
	2:00 – 5:00	Open house or buyer tour
	5:00 – 6:00	Listing presentation

But you're not a superstar yet. *30 Days to Dollars* takes the superstars' business principles and translates them to your situation:

- *Work your best source of prospects.* At this point, you have no past customers. But you do have a great network of people you know. Start with them.

- *Promote success.* Next, superstars create more success by promoting their success. If you are a new agent, find someone in your office who will let you promote yourself on his or her success—a new listing taken, a sale, a listing sold, an open house. This method is called *circle prospecting.* (Refer to Section 8 for an explanation of this process.)

- *Choose lead generating methods that match your style.* The *30 Days to Dollars* plan provides several methods for meeting prospects. But you can't reject all of them because you don't like any of them! Remember, it's a numbers game. (Refer to Section 8 for more information on these methods.) During the program, just do the four-week plan so you'll have the experience of making several kinds of sales calls, and you'll have met lots of people!

30 Days to Dollars translates these concepts that successful agents use to create high-producing businesses to your situation so that you can create the same kind of career base—quickly.

Caution: New agents fail because they start with the hardest, most expensive, smallest payoff lead-generating sources—which causes them to give up fast.

What about Cold-Calling?

Cold-calling means picking up the phone, dialing a stranger, and asking for a lead. Although cold-calling is the quickest way to get a lead if you're willing to make lots of sales calls, it isn't the most common way successful agents build their businesses. Why? The biggest reason is that real estate, over time, is a relationship continuance business. Agents just don't have the time and energy to get a new customer over and over. The second reason is that most successful agents are intuitive and emotional types. (The scientific name for this is *behavioral profile.* See the References section for more information.) They truly like people. They don't like to get a "no." They don't like the rejection they encounter making those hundreds of cold calls. They hate being rejected. They tend to get their feelings hurt! So, they avoid those situations where the likelihood of being rejected is high—situations like cold-calling.

Conversely, since they are intuitive and like to form and maintain relationships, they naturally enjoy working with those they know, and will work to maintain those relationships. The *30 Days to Dollars* plan, which does not include cold calls, is modeled after the *best sources* of business for the typical agent's "behavioral profile." Part of the reason these sources are prioritized as best is that most real estate agents like to do them and become good at them. So start with the best source of prospects—people who already know you. Remember: *the warmer the relationship, the better chance you have of getting a lead.*

What works. Too often agents want someone to give them one lead-generating method that is guaranteed to work. However, what always works is the numbers. Not only that—as you start selling, you'll discover that you are naturally drawn to certain types of lead generating, while you are repelled by others. That's your behavioral profile speaking! That's why we use a behavioral profile in our coaching company—to help people discover their best sources of business, and help them interact with people who have profiles that are different from theirs. In addition, relying on only one lead-generating method to pull you through even tough times is dangerous. Remember, again—it's a numbers game!

The pros and cons of cold-calling. Cold-calling does provide more contacts in the least amount of time. But it also brings more rejections and tougher contacts to convert. So, if you run out of people to talk to in the target markets recommended in *30 Days to Dollars*, go ahead and make cold calls—to anyone—using any method you want.

A script for cold-calling. A sales skill called craft a sales call script is described in Section 10. Using this technique, you can craft a sales call to any target market. If you want to cold-call in an area, just put together a script using this crafting technique. You will become a master cold caller because you not only have a script, you have the methodology behind the script. I've also put a script specifically designed for cold-calling in Section 13 for you, so you can cold-call as you need to.

If you don't know anyone. If you are new to your area, you will need to start with colder calls. However, before you begin cold-calling, take another look at the people you come in contact with weekly. Make a list of the service people you meet each week. Remember, every time you talk to someone, find out if he or she has a real estate need.

Look at cold-calling this way: it increases your repertoire. Being able to make several kinds of sales calls and mastering the sales skills in this program ensures that you have the repertoire.

But I don't wanna! Of course you don't want to do certain types of lead generating. But don't restrict yourself to only one type of lead generating—unless it is paying off big from the beginning. Develop the "chops" so you have them when you need them. Later in this section, I'll explain the numbers game: how many lead-generating contacts you must make weekly to get the weekly appointments you need to sell the number of homes you want to sell in a year.

Big Idea: Developing your lead-generating repertoire now will pay off when you need those skills and that confidence later.

It won't work for me in my area. If you find yourself saying that to an idea, an action, or a method I've given you in this resource, stop and ask yourself these questions:

- "Why am I resistant to this idea?"
- "How can I make this principle work for me?"
- "Is there something about my confidence level that's stopping me from taking this action?"
- "What am I trying to protect by being negative to this?"

In other words, don't throw the baby out with the bathwater! I am giving you the template, the process, the principles, the system, and the examples. I am giving you enough information for you to get started. You *can* improvise on this tune. The principles here are proven; this is a system. Use it as a basis to improvise.

Two Developments Demand That Agents Adapt to Changes

For the last few years, real estate agents, along with all salespeople, have had to change their cold-calling practices to comply with the law. In addition, real estate buyers' habits have changed. These two developments have had huge ramifications for agents. Let's look at the first challenge, the National Do Not Call Registry.

Leave me alone! On September 29, 2003, President Bush signed into law federal do-not-call legislation, and real estate professionals are expected to comply with the provisions of the National Do Not Call Registry. Most real estate companies have adapted their practices and procedures regarding the scope of this law. It is important to check with your broker to stay updated on this law and its rules. Information is also available on the National Association of REALTORS® Web site (*www.realtor.org*).

A Do-Not-Call/Do-Not-Fax Toolkit, with over 100 pages of information, is available to NAR members. With that amount of information available from a source that has been double-checked by your professional association's attorneys, you can see why I need not say more about it here!

The Internet buyer has created new communication challenges for agents. Remember those Internet buyers? They start their research on the Internet. Their time line for research is much longer than the non-Internet buyer's. According to a survey by Most Home Technologies, a lead follow-up service company, Internet buyers take 16.7 months from the time they start researching to the time they purchase. As sellers they take an average of 9.3 months. Only 4 to 8 percent of the leads obtained online close within 90 days. The rest stay in research for a long time.

Unfortunately, most agents are still in the "next" communication mode. They meet someone and think that person will buy from them in the next 30 days. If that person doesn't buy, they drop the person and go on to the next. They have neither the system nor the technology back-up to keep in contact with potential leads.

The good news about the Internet buyer. Once an Internet buyer finds an agent and starts looking at house, he or she again acts differently from a traditional buyer. Look at this research:

- *Decision-making time.* The traditional buyer, according to a recent California Association of REALTORS® study, takes seven weeks from the time they start looking at homes to the time they actually buy. The Internet buyer takes only two weeks. The reason it takes so much less time for the Internet buyer to make a decision is that they have educated themselves via their searches on the Internet. They don't have to look at so many homes "in the flesh."
- *Number of homes inspected.* The traditional buyer looks at over twice as many homes as the Internet buyer (because the traditional buyer hasn't done the research).
- *Choice of agent.* A vast majority of Internet buyers choose the agent with whom they formed a relationship and don't shop agents.

Today's Successful Agent Profile: Short-Term Lead Generator and Long-Term Communicator

New agents expect a sale quickly—more quickly than the Internet buyer typically buys. So you need to get into action quickly, using the *30 Days to Dollars* prioritized lead-generating plan. But to get a bigger payoff from all that lead generating in the future, you must

1. capture all your leads in your database so you won't lose them,
2. apply a contact management program so you'll follow up on your leads, and
3. make a marketing plan for these leads and drive it with your contact management (what you'll do to contact them and when you'll do it).

The best business strategy for the future. The successful agent of tomorrow will create a marketing program to keep in touch until their contacts "buy or die" so that when the Internet buyers are done with their research, the buyers and the agent will work exclusively together to make a quick buying decision.

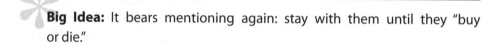

Big Idea: It bears mentioning again: stay with them until they "buy or die."

Business planning tip: Use the marketing plan explained in Section 9 to ensure you're not a "love 'em and leave 'em" short-term-thinking agent.

Remember the Relationship Marketing Trend

Your business start-up is based on the trend—and the marketing truism—that relationship marketing creates the most business in the shortest amount of time, with the least cost. In fact, relationship marketing has always been the method great salespeople use to create long-term business. Businesses internationally have discovered that it is the best way to market their businesses because it costs less and delivers better results.

An example of how companies have changed their strategy and their training is how car salespeople treat customers. A good car salesperson today actually keeps in touch with you after you have bought the car! Although that used to be rare, it's more common today because car company surveys have showed that people buy the same car again not because of mechanical service excellence but because they feel the people in the car dealership cared for them.

How many agents do you think keep in contact with the buyer and seller after the sale? Not many. In fact, a recent study showed that less than 40 percent of real estate agents ever contacted their buyers after closing! (So the buyer thinks we took the money and ran . . .) Many agents still think that their job is to find strangers and sell them something, then move on to the next stranger. Remember, it's nine times more expensive to advertise to find strangers (like by placing ads in newspapers) than it is to keep the old customer and get referrals.

> **Big Idea:** Communicate regularly with your best source of business (your clients and your sphere of influence).

Create your marketing plan and systematize it. Don't think that you can keep your relationships by ignoring the people you have talked to. You must create a marketing plan to "re-touch" them regularly. One of your business-supporting assignments will be to create that marketing plan and do a marketing action weekly. In Section 9, I'll give you information on how to create a marketing plan, along with a sample plan and a marketing planner that covers all the bases.

Use technology to systematize your marketing plan. After you've made your marketing plan, systematize it by putting it in your contact management system. Now the system will remind you when to implement the action you've planned.

Many companies will provide postcards and mailing services to keep in touch. See your manager or company catalog for lists of these companies and services. You can easily create a call/postcard program to let these people know you care about them. If you prefer creating a program yourself, see senior agents in your office. They can help you create simple postcards with current or sold listings. You can also send flyers or brochures of homes you've recently listed and sold. At first, your list will be small, so write a personal note on each mailing to let the buyers and sellers know you are thinking about them. Companies like the Personal Marketing Company, QuantumMail.com, Sensations, and Prospects Plus all have affordable marketing programs that are "turn-key." (See Section 14, References, for more information.)

What Information Do You Need?

You will need the following information about your contacts:

- All of the person's contact data, including e-mail and Web site information. It's especially important today to get e-mail addresses so you can send updates and newsletters electronically.
- Personal preferences and personal information, such as birthdays, children's names, pets' names, and so on.
- Information regarding each transaction.

> **Big Idea:** Get into the habit of "meet up, put them in your database, and contact them"—all within one day of meeting them, so you won't lose those precious contacts, and they won't forget you!

Real estate–specific programs like Top Producer and Online Agent already have these fields built into their programs. For a person new to real estate or databases, these customized databases are useful. The downside is that the real estate–specific programs are more expensive. (See more information on these programs in the References section.)

Two other bonuses that real estate specific programs offer are

1. Letters for many contact occasions and
2. Marketing plans for specific target markets (identifiable groups of people with common needs) such as people selling their own homes ("for sale by owners") or people who have tried to sell their homes through real estate agents but failed ("expired listings").

A fellow board member of an Internet training company that specializes in online real estate training—and a founder of the largest contact management software company for real estate professionals—tells me that agents who buy his programs use only a fraction of the features. He also knows a top-producing agent who closes about $20 million of properties a year and has been lauded for his innovative marketing programs. In fact, all this agent is doing is using the programs provided in his software!

As a new agent, unless you are very contact management–savvy and have been in sales before, I caution you against using a generic contact management program. Instead, buy real estate–specific software and learn all the features. Use the letters and marketing programs in the software until you are comfortable customizing them and/or creating your own programs. Using these programs will be a self-training tool. Take advantage of the thousands of hours of expertise that went into creating those programs for real estate agents!

 Big Idea: It's better to start with *any* database than with none.

Lead Generation: *30 Days to Dollars* Prioritizes Your Best Sources

Agents who didn't learn the business with the *Up and Running* concepts constantly ask me, "What are the best sources of leads?" In this program, I have given you the answers. I have prioritized the best sources of leads for the new real estate agent. *30 Days to Dollars* (see Figure 2.4) is the most important part of your *Up and Running* program. Why? Because it is the lead-generating plan component of *Up and Running in 30 Days*. It consists of the following:

- Your **best sources of business**, prioritized for you
- The **numbers of contacts** you need to make
- The **time frame** in which you need to make them

It is structured to ensure a sale in your first 30 days in the business. Take another look at *30 Days to Dollars* (Figure 2.4). You'll see four sources of leads and the numbers of contacts recommended per week in each source. Those are the sources you'll be using to get leads during these four weeks. But you won't be contacting all those sources in week one. That would be overwhelming! You'll start with one source and keep adding sources. Each week, a new source of leads will be introduced to you so you can expand your repertoire for getting leads. Doing the numbers of contacts recommended in this plan gets you a sale in a month.

Big Idea: Your four-week plan introduces you to the lead-generating sources gradually so you can build your repertoire.

Why I Have Chosen These Lead-Generating Priorities

Too many lead-generating plans are just an unprioritized laundry list of all the things you could do to generate business. I don't want you to waste time and energy pursuing sources that don't give you a high payoff. I have chosen those activities because they are perfect for new agents. They are *low cost,* both in energy and money. Best of all, they're *high payoff.* So I've created this *30 Days to Dollars* prioritized lead-generation plan with the new agent specifically in mind. In addition, my research with experienced agents shows that the best source of business is always *people they've sold to and people they've met.* Because you've not sold any real estate, I will give you your best source in your terms:

People you know or meet

Now, you know that this 30-day plan is just not for 30 days. It is a prioritized plan that should last you your whole real estate career! In other words, it is a model for the successful real estate agent.

Big Idea: Know your best lead-generating sources.

FIGURE 2.4   *30 Days to Dollars* Lead-Generating Plan

These lead-generating activities are assigned in a prioritized order each week of your four-week plan.

Lead-Generating Source		Weekly Minimum
1. Contact people you know/meet (best source)		
	In-person calls	20
	Phone calls	30
2. Circle prospect in person (next best source for new agents)		25
3. FSBOs	In-person or phone contacts	25
or		
Expired listings	In-person or phone contacts	25
4. Hold public open houses		1

Total weekly minimum in-person/phone contacts to get a sale in your first month:  **100–125**

Why "People You Know" Is Top Priority

Simply, these people already like and trust you! They want to do business with you. They just don't know you're in real estate. Your job is to contact them, let them know you're in real estate, and ask for their business—or referrals (see Section 8 for the process and script). There are four other reasons why this source is your best:

1. It is very low cost with high return.
2. It requires little skill.
3. It is inexpensive.
4. You have no competition for this market—these people already love you!

Why Circle Prospecting Is Next Highest Priority

Circle prospecting means going door to door in a neighborhood to announce a "home happening"—that is, a new listing, a sale, a listing sold, a price reduction, an open house, or a closing. (See Section 8 for how to circle prospect.) There are four reasons why circle prospecting is so powerful for the new agent:

1. It is easy to do—it requires little skill.
2. It is "low rejection"—most homeowners are glad you informed them.
3. It is inexpensive.
4. It has little competition—most agents will not bother to personally contact homeowners.

Why For-Sale-by-Owner and Expired Listings Are Lower Priority

For-sale-by-owner listings, or listings by owners attempting to sell their own homes, and expired listings, listings that didn't sell, can be *immediate sources* of business. Why? Because these sellers have told us they want to sell. That's the good news. The bad news is that these sellers don't have a high opinion of real estate salespeople. Perhaps they've had a bad experience in the past and decided that selling their own homes is preferable than working with a bad agent. Perhaps they had their home listed by an unscrupulous agent who overpriced it just to get calls on the sign. The reason that I've prioritized these sources as third on the list is that they

1. require skill,
2. are high-rejection sales activities, and
3. require you to have the kind of behavioral profile to accept and deal with high rejection and tough sellers—and stay in the game! Only about one-fourth of the population is "wired" that way. See more on behavioral profiles in *Become Tomorrow's Mega-Agent Today!*

We will teach you how to contact these best sources of business. Information on contacting and working with these sources is in Section 8. See the References section for much more help on sales skills.

Why Open Houses Are Included

The first three sources are "proactive." That is, you go out and contact these sources. This puts you in the driver's seat, because you have control over the number of people you contact. The last source, open houses, is "reactive." That is, you sit and wait for a potential client. You can't make them come to your open house (but you can up the odds by putting out more signs). You can also up the odds by circle prospecting around that home a day before the open house. I've included open houses here because new agents generally have many opportunities to hold homes open. Before you commit to an open house, though, be sure it is in a well-trafficked area and that you have access to plenty of open house signs (most people come as a result of well-placed signs, not ads). Caution: you need sales training to ask the right questions during your open house to capture that lead.

Big Idea: Recognize whether you are lead generating proactively or reactively.

Other Reactive Sales Activities

You may be accepting Internet leads. You may be getting leads from your relocation service (or *relo*). This is a service, usually owned by your real estate company, that has affiliate relationships with national or international relocation services. These services interact to find and provide leads to real estate agencies, who then distribute them to agents—for a fee, which ranges from 20 percent to 45 percent. You may be working as a buyer's agent and getting leads from your head agent. These are all reactive sources. If you don't intend to hold open houses, you can substitute your other reactive sources instead. A huge caveat: do not expect to create a career from reactive sources. If that were true, every agent in the business would be making the money of his dreams!

How These Priorities Are Introduced During the Program

Figure 2.5 shows you when each new lead-generating source is introduced to you during your *Up and Running* plan. Take a quick peek at Sections 4–7. Look at the action plans for week one, week two, week three, and week four. You'll see your lead-generating assignments there, just as they show up in Figure 2.5.

FIGURE 2.5   Time Line: When New Lead-Generating Activities Are Introduced

---

Each week during the *Up and Running* plan you will be lead generating at least 100 contacts. Here's the schedule of when *Up and Running* introduces and expects these lead-generating sources to be implemented:

Week One	Week Two	Week Three	Week Four
People you know	Add expireds	Add FSBOs	You choose
Circle prospecting	Continue people you know	Continue people you know	
	Continue circle prospecting	Continue circle prospecting	

More sources are added to your lead-generating plan assignments in each week of the program. We start with the best and easiest sources for you, and progress to the more difficult (requiring more sales training) sources. By the time you've been in the business four weeks, you've sampled the major types of lead-generating activities. And, you've done them in high enough numbers to see your results. In addition, you've found which sources you like best—and which bring you the best results. Now, longer term, you can put into your plan more work in these best sources. At the same time, because you've practiced the sales skills of all the major sources (by lead generating in real life), you have the skills to implement any of these sources any time you need them. Remember, it's first a numbers game!

Big Idea: Sales is a numbers game.

Other Sources of Leads

I have created an area called "other" on your *30 Days to Dollars* spreadsheet. If you have other favored sources of leads, set goals and track them there. Be sure to categorize them as proactive or reactive. Remember, proactive leads put you in control, because you're going out to find the lead. Reactive (e.g., open houses, floor time, Internet leads given to you, and Relo leads) are not numbers that you control.

What about Paying for Leads?

Today, there are a multitude of companies asking agents to pay them for leads. Should you do that? Perhaps. But before you leap into the fray, find out the following information.

Internet leads: you need a long-term approach and a great "screening" method. Here's what the Internet lead company surveys show. One company who sells leads to agents, HouseValues, says 40 percent of the leads they provide make a buying decision within 28 months. The founder of the company, Mark Powell, notes that most agents do not follow up for the amount of time it takes to convert the lead. Lead-generating company owners I've talked with are frustrated that agents expect a "sure thing" with these leads. However, Home Technologies, a lead follow-up service, says that only one out of 200 leads is converted to a sale. That means that you'd better be ready to

1. have a rapid response to Internet or any lead-giving inquiries, especially if you're paying for them;

2. implement a fail-safe contact management system to capture all those leads and categorize them;

3. have a tight, systematized follow-up plan for all those leads; and

4. have the skills to convert that Internet inquiry into a client (see Section 8 for Internet sales skills).

Caveat: be careful of accepting leads as your major source of business! For example, one newer agent got one-third of her business from her company's relocation service. She paid 40 percent of her commission to get those leads. In a fast market, she did pretty well. However, when the market slowed down, she got many fewer relo leads, and hadn't implemented her own lead-generating plan. So she never really created her business. She was simply the recipient of the company's relo business. She found herself really as a "day one" new agent—no business! So, she had to start from scratch and proactively lead generate. Don't let that happen to you. Just think of the marketing power and real estate business she would have had if she spent 40 percent of her commission dollars marketing to her best sources of business instead of accepting those relo leads.

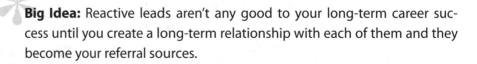

Big Idea: Reactive leads aren't any good to your long-term career success until you create a long-term relationship with each of them and they become your referral sources.

Substituting Lead-Generating Activities

What if you don't know enough people to fill a week with 50 contacts from this source? Just choose another source. The number of people you contact is the most important factor in your plan's success What you can't do: have low lead-generating numbers and expect sales!

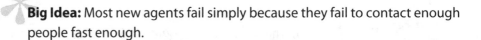

Big Idea: Most new agents fail simply because they fail to contact enough people fast enough.

The Spreadsheets: How the *30 Days to Dollars* Lead-Generating Plan Looks Each Week

I've taken the *30 Days to Dollars* plan in *Up and Running* and put it in a spreadsheet format for you so you can see your lead-generating assignments (your goals) and track your results (actuals). Look at Figures 2.6 and 2.7. Figure 2.6 shows you the lead-generating sources you are assigned

Resource: Software to Generate These Numbers for You— and More

If you would like to put your goals into a spreadsheet using your computer and keep your results, we have a resource for you at Carla Cross Seminars, Inc. Our *Up and Running* CD package now comes with what we call a "document CD," which has the *Up and Running* forms with your goals for business-producing and business-supporting activities already entered in a format you can use on your computer. Get more information in the References section.

each week. In this example, the agent has done every part of the plan. Figure 2.7 shows you the sales activity this agent generated as a result of his lead-generating work. These are the projections for you during the four weeks. Now flip ahead for a minute to Section 4. You will see that your first week's lead-generating assignments are the same as the ones for week one on your spreadsheet. This is to make it easy for you to follow a proven start-up plan, so you won't have to figure out priorities or needed numbers. You will also see that your result projections are stated as goals for you in week one. Although we can't guarantee results, working these high lead-generating numbers will ultimately result in sales for you much faster than if you had started with a "slow" plan!

Blank spreadsheets are provided for you to use each week in Section 12. I've already put in the lead-generating assignments and results projections to make it easy for you to keep your results.

Track Your Results and Make Adjustments

Each week, use the spreadsheets to track your results. Look at the results you're getting from your lead generating and make adjustments in your plan. I'll share much more about that in the *Up and Running* plan.

After *Up and Running* Is Over

Don't stop using those spreadsheets! At the end of four weeks, you'll see which have been your best sources of business. Now, you're ready to make your own plan from scratch using the principles you've already learned.

Best advice: don't make your own plan your first four weeks. Use my plan until you get the success habits you need to succeed. Then you can alter the plan.

■ Principle Five: Work the Numbers

Do you want to make a sale in your first month in the business? If so, you need to make at least 100 lead-generating contacts (in person or on the phone) each week for the first four weeks you're in the business. This is your insurance plan. The *30 Days to Dollars* lead-generating plan has 100 contacts per week built into the program. But, you say, that's a lot of contacts. Yes, but you want to sell a home quickly, don't you? And you have plenty of time to make those contacts, don't you? And you don't have enough money not to sell a home soon. Finally, you want to keep your enthusiasm high, don't you? Those are all the reasons to make those contacts.

So, get to it. You will use and assess this program each week. With this method, you will learn an important self-management tool—the ability to measure and analyze your activities, and the results of those activities.

FIGURE 2.6   Your *30 Days to Dollars* Lead-Generating Plan

Set your goals and track your results ("actuals")

Month: _____

	Week 1 G	Week 1 A	Week 2 G	Week 2 A	Week 3 G	Week 3 A	Week 4 G	Week 4 A	Totals G	Totals A
Proactive Activities										
People you know/meet [50/week]	(50)	50	(25)	25	(25)	25	25	25	125	125
Circle prospect [25/week]	(50)	50	50	50	(25)	25	25	25	150	150
FSBOs [25/week]	0	0	0	0	(25)	25	25	25	75	75
Expireds [25/week]	0	0			25*	(25)	25*	25	50	50
Reactive Activities										
Open houses [1 minimum]	0	0	(1)	1	(1)	1	(1)	1	3	3

G=Goals
A=Actuals

Circled are the numbers of lead-generating activities from each source—in the specific week they are assigned in your *Up and Running* plan.

*By Week 3, you get to choose your favorite methods among those listed.

FIGURE 2.7 Your *30 Days to Dollars* Lead-Generating Results

Month: _____

Buyer Activities

	Week 1		Week 2		Week 3		Week 4		Totals	
	G	A	G	A	G	A	G	A	G	A
Qualifying interviews w/buyers	2	2	2	2	2	2	2	2	8	8
Qualified buyer showings	2	2	2	2	2	2	2	2	8	8
# sales							1	1	1	1

Listing Activities

	Week 1		Week 2		Week 3		Week 4		Totals	
	G	A	G	A	G	A	G	A	G	A
Qualified listing appointments	1	1	1	1	1	1	1	1	4	4
Marketable listings secured	0	0	0	0	0	0	1	1	1	1
# of listings sold	0	0	0	0	0	0	0	0	0	0*

G=Goals   A=Actuals

Note the results projected through time. These results are in your four-week *Up and Running* plan.

*Depends on your normal market time.

More Numbers: High Activities Reap High Rewards

The majority of new agents have no faith that the activities they are doing on any given day will bring them results. That's because they don't know the *Up and Running* plan. Here are the very important contact ratios you need to learn so you will know that you are doing what it takes to succeed.

On the sales side,

- 400 contacts per month will return to you
- 8 qualifying appointments that will result in
- 8 showings that, if averaged over time, will result in 1 sale.

This means if you want to sell one home per month, you need to talk to 400 people in that month, find 8 people to qualify, and show homes 8 times. You will, averaged over a few months, sell 1 home for every 8 times you put people in the car (not necessarily the same people—this is just a law of averages).

On the listing side,

- 400 contacts a month will result in
- 4 seller-qualifying appointments that will lead to
- 1 qualified listing.

The *Up and Running* plan has these numbers built into each week's business-producing activities. You will set a goal for *one sale and one listing* during the first four weeks of your business. In addition, you'll be setting standards for your business that will ensure you will make a good living and build a solid career—from day one. As we progress in *Up and Running,* I'll remind you to review your ratios to make certain you are doing the lead generating and getting the appointment numbers you need to reach your goals.

■ Principle Six: Be Accountable to Your Plan

Don't just write some numbers and forget about it. Write your goals, and track your actual activities and results. That's how you learn to control your income. Through analyzing your own success ratios, you'll be able to truly self-manage.

One of the questions new agents always ask is, "How much work will I have to do?" *Up and Running* certainly lays that out, doesn't it? But that's not the whole story. You just saw the ratios above. But those aren't yours. Ratios can vary dramatically. For example:

1. George goes into the business with a mastery of sales skills. When he makes a sales call, it takes him fewer calls to get a lead than it does Sally, who came into this business without any sales skills.
2. Martha goes into this business, and, although she knows lots of people, is reluctant to talk to them about real estate. Instead, Martha, who is very sociable and hates rejection, decides to call on for-sale-by-owner listings. She experiences high rejection, so she decides she doesn't like real estate. Her ratio of calls to leads is terrible!
3. It's a very fast market in Seattle when Chris starts in the business. He finds it very easy to get a lead and very easy to sell that lead a house because the lead is afraid he'll lose the house if he doesn't buy today! In contrast, John starts selling in Florida in a very slow market. John has to make many sales calls to find a good lead.

So quit worrying about my conversion ratios. Start tracking your leads, appointments, and sales. Find *your* conversion ratios. As a musician, I practiced as long as it took to play well. I've never understood the kind of person who thinks she'll just do enough to get by. High achievers don't think like that. Aim high! You're worth it.

■ *Up and Running:* A Start-Up Plan Built in the Six Principles

With these six principles, you have the groundwork of an effective start-up plan. But you don't have to create your plan from scratch. To make it easy for you to launch your business, I've done it for you. *Up and Running* provides a highly structured four-week plan built on those principles (see Sections 4–7). The plan includes the *30 Days to Dollars* lead-generating plan (business-producing activities) and the business-supporting actions you'll want to take to become great at sales—and package your presentations so you can compete with seasoned agents.

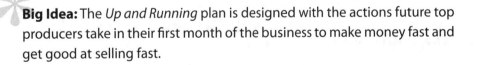

Big Idea: The *Up and Running* plan is designed with the actions future top producers take in their first month of the business to make money fast and get good at selling fast.

How the *Up and Running* Plan Gets You to Your Goals

The *Up and Running* four-week plan tells you what to do from your first week in the business to ensure you start your business fast—and right. That's the short-term, immediate look at your business. But how is it going to extend to get you to your yearly goals? Now I'll show you how it's built to *continue* to get you the results you want in your first year. Figure 2.8 is a yearly goal planner, filled out by our *Up and Running* agent.

First, I want to show you the relationship between your yearly goals and what you do today. This goal-setting planner helps you set your year's goals, and in addition, it breaks your goals into monthly goals and the *specific activities* you need to do every day to achieve those goals (broken down by the month). Look at month one. You'll see our *Up and Running* plan numbers for the first month. Now, look at month two. See how the number of contacts goes down a bit as the results remain steady. That is how you continue your *Up and Running* plan through time. The activities you do those first few months get you the sales and listings sold you want at the end of the year. Look at the rest of the figure, which shows the relationship between your activities and your results.

Big Idea: The activities you do those first few months get you the sales and listings sold you want at the end of the year. There's a *direct* relationship!

Goals without Knowing What to Do Every Day Is Useless

Activities → Goals

To have faith in a plan, you want to know how the activities you do today ensures the results you get at the end of that year. Most new agents can tell someone how much money they want to make their first year, but they have no idea what they're going to do every day to make it! I found that out when I surveyed hundreds of new agents for my book *Become Tomorrow's Mega-Agent Today!* You need both views of your business—short term and long term—to launch into these activities so you have confidence in your ability to reach your goals.

Caution: Agents fail because they don't create an activity plan to support their goals.

Steps to Set Your Goals

1. Plan your yearly goals
2. Break down yearly goals into monthly goals/actions
3. Create a weekly schedule that reflects your monthly goals and actions
4. Create your budget
5. Forecast your profits

The Five Steps to Create Your Effective Yearly Plan

So you can project your success one year from now, here are the steps to create your yearly plan. I've put a sample of all of the completed *Up and Running* plan forms in Section 11, so you can see how all the forms filled

FIGURE 2.8 Yearly Goals and Monthly Activities

1. Set your monthly expections

Your $ expectations this year

| $ 72,000 | ÷ 12 = | $ 6,000 |

Monthly expectation in $

2. Translate $ to revenue units*
   * "units" are numbers of sales and listings sold

Monthly expectation in $

| $ 6,000 | ÷ | $ 6,000 | = | 1/2 | 1/2 |

Your $ earned sale per listing sold

Monthly unit goal

Listings sold   Sales

3. Plan activities to meet revenue unit goals using the numbers and ratios in *Up and Running*

| | **Month** | | | | | |
	1	2	3	4	5	6
Listings Sold	0	0	1	0	1	0
Listings Taken	1	0	1	0	0	1
Listing Appts.	4	4	4	4	4	4
Sales	1	1	0	1	0	1
Showing Appts.	8	8	8	8	8	8
Contacts (From *30 Days to $*)	400	300	200	200	200	200

The first month activities coincide with the *Up and Running* plan. Our agent follows the same contact plan she used for her third month onward to schedule her contacts and business results for the remainder of the year.

out work together. I've put all the blank forms you'll need to plan and measure your short-term and long-term results in Section 12 for you and on my *Up and Running* CD (see References):

1. Plan your yearly goals (see the sample plan in Figure 2.8)
2. Break down your yearly goals into monthly goals and actions (a blank form of your yearly goals and monthly activity plan is in Section 12)
3. Create a weekly schedule that reflects your monthly goals and actions so your goals are really your action plan (I'll give you a sample weekly schedule and a method to create an effectively weekly schedule in Section 4, Week One)
4. Create your budget (see the sample budget in Figure 2.9 and the blank budget planning sheet in Section 12)
5. Forecast your profits (see the sample forecast in Figure 2.10 and the blank forecast in Section 12)

1. Plan your yearly goals. Let's work from your yearly goals to the activities you'll need to do and results you want to achieve each month. First, using Figure 2.8, the *Up and Running* agent sets her monetary goal for the year. For her, that's $72,000 her first year in real estate. (This, by the way, is higher than the median income for all REALTORS® according to the latest National Association of REALTORS® survey. I'm assuming that you intend to really work at real estate in a planned way to exceed the median.) Because the average income per sale for the agent in her market is $6,000, this means that she'll need to sell one home per month (or have one of her listings sell). In the real estate industry, each sale or listing sold is termed a "revenue unit." You will note that she will create one-half a revenue unit per month from a sale and a listing sold.

2. Break down yearly goals into monthly goals and actions. This *Up and Running* agent went to her manager and found out that, in her area, it takes approximately four listing appointments to list one home that sells in normal market time. It takes eight showing appointments to sell one home. This means eight groups of people in the car, not numbers of homes shown. They don't even have to be different groups; it's just the law of averages. Because our *Up and Running* agent wants one transaction per month, she knows she will have to put people in her car and go to a listing presentation at least four times per month to ensure that she reaches her goal. As she knows her fastest method of getting a check is through a sale, she sets a goal of eight showings per month. She also knows that her skill level isn't high at the beginning of her career, so she sets higher showing and listing presentation goals for herself than she will need to set later in her career.

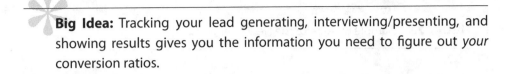

Big Idea: Tracking your lead generating, interviewing/presenting, and showing results gives you the information you need to figure out *your* conversion ratios.

Big Idea: If you want to make lots of money your first year in real estate, you must lead generate your heart out every day!

3. Create a weekly schedule that reflects your monthly goals and actions. Here's where the rubber meets the road. Your plan is not a practical tool for you to use unless it directs you in what to do each week—and every day. Your *Up and Running* four-week plan gives you the specifics— what to do each week to reach your goals. In week one of your plan, you'll be putting together your weekly schedule based on the activities in the plan for week one. There is an example schedule for week one in Section 11. After you've gained the time management skills in *Up and Running*, you'll be able to make your own weekly schedule.

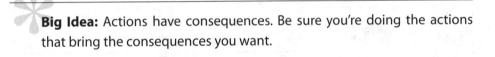

Big Idea: Actions have consequences. Be sure you're doing the actions that bring the consequences you want.

4. Create your budget. Figure 2.9 provides a sample budget for the new agent. You will get some budget numbers, too, from your Technology Planner. Knowing what you need to close each month is a motivator to get out there and lead generate!

5. Forecast your income. Figure 2.10 is an example time line, which shows you the *Up and Running* plan sales results for each month, plus your outgo (the budgeted dollars you're spending each month to launch your career). To find out more about what you should be spending, see your manager. Costs vary greatly from area to area, and your company may provide many or none of the materials and services you need to launch your career. (See the References section for much more on budgeting and projections.)

FIGURE 2.9   Sample Budget for the New Agent

Your Real Estate Budget
Real Estate Operating Expenses

Projections: 6 sales this year

           6 listings sold this year

           8 listings taken this year

	YEARLY	MONTHLY
Total marketing budget ($200 per listing/sale)	$2,800	$233
Professional fees (REALTORS, MLS)	600	50
Business car expenses (gas, oil, tools, repair)	2,400	200
Communication expenses (pager, phone)	1,200	100
Labor/mechanical	1,200	100
Professional development	600	50
Supplies	1,200	100
Business insurance	300	25
Legal fees / E&O	300	25
Licenses, permits	300	25
Other	1,200	100
TOTAL	$12,100	$1,008

FIGURE 2.10   Sample Budget Forecast for Year One

Month	1	2	3	4	5	6	7	8	9	10	11	12
Sales	1	1										
Listings Sold			1	1	1	1	1		1		1	1
Income (closings)		6,000*	6,000	6,000	6,000	6,000	6,000	6,000	6,000	6,000	6,000	6,000
Expenses Out	1,008	1,008	1,008	1,008	1,008	1,008	1,008	1,008	1,008	1,008	1,008	1,008
Profit	(1,008)	4,992	4,992	4,992	4,992	4,992	4,992	4,992	4,992	4,992	4,992	4,992

Total income: $66,000
Total expenses: − $12,100
Profit: $53,900

*Note: If you make a sale in month one, that sale will be in month two, when the home closes. There is also a month lag from a sold listing to a closing.

Breakeven. Figure 2.10 shows you when your income and outgo are at "breakeven." This usually happens in an agent's business by the fourth to sixth month.

What happens if you don't start lead generating *now*? Very simply, your money will run out before enough of your income comes in!

Caution: Too many new agents fail because they run out of money and time just before they get that first sale!

From Unpredictable to Predictable Results

Now go back to Figure 2.8. Note the *Up and Running* agent doesn't get a sale or a listing sold every month at first. Why? Because she's generating hundreds of leads, some who won't buy from her in the first few months. However, she's sowing the seeds of success by contacting those hundreds of people. In addition, at first this new agent, like most new agents, has few sales skills. It takes her more contacts to get a good prospect. As her sales skills and the quality of her contacts grow, she'll enjoy more success with less effort.

Big Idea: Predictability comes with repetition.

Don't Concentrate on the Results; Concentrate on the Activities

New agents expect to make a sale fast. However, they don't know the work required to make that sale. You do now. But don't be tempted to think that because you said you wanted to make a sale in the first month, you will! Stop thinking about those sales. Instead, concentrate on those lead-generating activities. Remember, your friend the new agent may make a sale in his first month because of dumb luck. That won't happen often. The worst thing about dumb luck is that it makes the agent think all he has to do is sit around and someone will force the agent to sell him a home. I've seen many new agents who had that dumb luck early in their careers, and that's the last home they ever sold! Selling isn't magic. It's work.

Big Idea: New agents fail because they have no plan—and take no focused action—to get to their goals.

Your Lead-Generating Plan after Your First Month

Notice that the *Up and Running* agent reduces the number of contacts she's making after her first month. That's because she is getting the number of leads she needs to convert them to the number of appointments she needs—and ultimately, the number of sales and listings sold. By month three, she's learned that she needs 200 contacts a month to get the appointments she needs to reach her goal for the number of sales and listings sold annually. How does she know these ratios? She has tracked her goals and actuals and analyzed her progress. You should do the same with the spreadsheets I've provided you. That way, you won't be guessing at whether you are on track to your goals or not. You'll know!

How Many Lead-Generating Hours after Your First Month?

This *Up and Running* agent now knows she doesn't need to devote four hours a day five days a week to lead generating anymore. She now has appointments to schedule. So, she reduces the amount of hours she lead generates a week to ten and continues to do that throughout her career.

If the *Up and Running* Agent Hits a Slump

Too many times, agents stop lead generating because they "get too busy," and then they find they are in a slump. Unfortunately, few of them started with the clarity of an *Up and Running* plan, so they don't really know why they're in the slump. It's different when you start with *Up and Running*. If our *Up and Running* agent doesn't reach her monthly sales goals, she knows exactly what to correct. She knows her conversion ratios—the number of leads she must get to interview, the number of showings she must get to sell, and the number of listing appointments she must make to get a marketable listing. So, she cures her "slumpitis" by increasing her lead generation to three to four hours a day, contacting 300 to 400 people a week again. That's your cure, too!

Big Idea: Slumps are caused by inaction or wrong actions.

■ All Your Self-Management Tools Are Here

1. *30 Days to Dollars*—provides a monthly and weekly lead-generating plan and spreadsheets to track activities on the sales cycle

2. *Your yearly goals and monthly activity plan*—plans your one-year goals so you can then plan your month and your week—even your day

3. *Up and Running budget*—so you can budget enough dollars to start your career right

4. *Budget forecast*—shows the relationship of income to expenses, and when you break even

All of these blank forms for your use are in Section 12.

■ Summary

We explored what I've identified as the six major principles of a high-producing business and what they mean to you:

1. *Start the business cycle by talking to people.* Unfortunately, most new agents wait months to start lead generating. They are frightened, feel the need for more education, or are looking for a "better way." In fact, they wait themselves right out of the business! If you want to make a sale in your first month, you need to start lead generating *your first day in the business.*

2. *Stay on the business path.* That means you should spend the majority of your day doing business-producing activities: lead generating and working with buyers and sellers. Unfortunately, most new agents spend most of their day getting ready to get ready!

3. *Prioritize your activities.* I have come up with the concept of prioritizing all activities as either business producing or business supporting. Now you have the skills to direct your own activities toward—or away from—productivity. But I haven't left it up to you. I've scheduled you for your first month so you will have complete clarity of what a successful real estate agent does every day to succeed.

4. *Lead generate like the pros.* My 30-day prioritized lead-generating plan, *30 Days to Dollars,* shows you which are your best sources for leads and how many of them you must contact each week to get a sale your first month. I don't want to leave it up to you to decide on your lead-generating sources. One new agent in my office thought that if he just sent out postcards to those he knew, he would sell lots of houses. Wrong!

5. *Work the numbers.* Too many times, agents tell me they "tried that once." It's a numbers game! Trying something once is just telling me you really aren't committed. What if you wanted to learn to play the piano, yet you practiced only once? Keep working those numbers. You'll get better at sales. You'll see your progress get faster. Analyze your numbers so you can self-manage.

6. *Be accountable to your plan.* Treat your plan with respect. Measure your actual activities and results against what this plan projects. Find your own conversion ratios. Now you're on your way to creating the kind of business results you want—and you now have the skills to measure and adjust your plan as needed. I'll let you in on a secret, too: you know 98 percent more about managing your business than other agents—no matter how long they've been in the business. Just think what you're going to accomplish!

Big Idea: These principles aren't just for "newbies." These principles are for every type of salesperson building and maintaining a career.

Now, let's go on to Section 3 to get the overview of the *Up and Running* plan so you can start your week one.

Four Weeks to Becoming a Successful Agent

In the previous section, you learned the six principles of successful business development. These principles are the ones I used to create the *Up and Running* four-week plan. Sections 4 through 7 are the plan, a week at a time, along with the measurement tools you and your manager need to manage your plan.

In this section, I'll give you a successful new agent's job description so you can see the job you are filling. Your *Up and Running* plan makes this job description "live" in your actions each day. You'll get an overview of the plan to get you ready for Section 4, your first week of the plan. In addition, we'll talk about management. You may not think you're in management because you're a new agent. But you really are, because you must manage your plan, while also managing your *attitude*. For most new agents, the hardest part of implementing this plan is managing their attitudes! I'll give you some pointers about enlisting your manager in your plan and some suggestions if you're working with a coach so you can get the best results possible. Finally, I'll give you checklist of the materials you need as you enter the business so you're ready to get started selling real estate. Then you're all set to start your plan.

■ What a Successful New Real Estate Agent Does

When you apply for a job, you're generally given a job description so you know what's expected of you. Were you given a job description when you applied to become a real estate salesperson? Probably not. No wonder few new real estate salespeople know what to expect when they started their careers! No wonder they often get their priorities wrong and unwittingly create a business plan for failure! Figure 3.1 is my job description for a successful agent. Notice that it's prioritized using the categories from *Up and Running*. Not all activities are equal. That's exactly what the *Up and Running* plan teaches, too. As you start your *Up and Running* plan with week one, your are fulfilling this job description, just as those who fail are fulfilling a "failed agent" job description. Keep my job description at your desk in front of you to remind you of your priorities.

Big Idea: What you do each day creates your job description.

Manager's Tip: Give this job description to each new agent candidate during the interview. Ask each if he is willing to do this job description. You'll weed out those who aren't interested in being successful.

FIGURE 3.1   A Successful Agent's Job Description

A successful agent consistently completes large numbers of business-producing activities:

1. Lead generates. Finds potential customers and clients by lead generating with the best sources daily.

   An agent's income is greatly determined by the number of people contacted consistently.

2. Completes a high number of these activities:
   - Shows homes to qualified customers
   - Sells homes
   - Lists marketable properties to sell in normal market time

3. Makes money by
   - Selling homes
   - Selling listings

   (The only two activities that get you a paycheck)

4. Completes support activities with lower priority:
   - Preview properties
   - Paperwork/sales follow-up
   - Education/training/coaching
   - Meetings
   - Marketing

■ The Priorities of *Up and Running*

The most important part of *Up and Running* is the *30 Days to Dollars* prioritized lead-generating plan. During your first 30 days, you will do the following:

- Complete 400 proactive lead-generating contacts with the priorities of *30 Days to Dollars*
- Get eight qualified appointments to show
- Get one sale
- Get four listing appointments
- Get one marketable listing

Doing these actions in the order and number assigned will get you into production fast. But that's not all you need to do to sell lots of houses.

Business-Supporting Activities Give You Sales Mastery

Besides making those sales calls and doing presentations, plus showing and listing homes, you need to develop your skills. Why? You'll be working smarter, not harder. Why go to ten listing presentations to get one marketable listing if you could go to four to get one? You'll increase your success ratios by practicing and packaging to become a competent salesperson fast. That way, you'll be able to compete with salespeople who have been in the business much longer than you. In addition, you'll have the self-confidence to tackle any sales situation, knowing you have the sales skills and sales packaging to go into the fray and compete with the best. I've chosen the business-supporting activities because you need them *right now!* I haven't chosen myriad other activities because you don't need them right now to succeed in the short term. Here are the business-supporting actions you will complete:

Sales presentations
- Create a visual listing presentation and process so you can prove you're worth the commission you want to charge, and you can get a listing at a marketable price
- Design a buyer qualifying/counseling presentation and process so you can create buyer loyalty and get the commissions you feel you deserve

Time management and professional advancement tools
- Create and evaluate your weekly schedule
- Implement the Property Salability Questionnaire (set your standards and qualify sellers)
- Implement the Buyer's Potential Evaluator (set your standards and qualify buyers)

Tracking and contacting potential buyers and aellers
- Implement Tracking Qualified Buyers for time management
- Consistently enter contacts into your database
- Create a contact management system
- Complete your marketing plan and implement it weekly
- Follow up with all potential buyers and sellers

Technical skills and knowledge
- Complete a listing form
- Do a market analysis
- Complete four purchase and sale agreements
- Learn the basics of financing and qualifying

Sales skills
- Observe your office's floor time (or observe an agent answering phone inquiries)
- Observe open houses
- Practice the four lead-generating scripts
- Practice the seven critical sales skills

Why these particular sales skills? Because these skills are the ones you must master *right now* to convert leads to sales.

But How Do I Make Those Contacts and Work with Buyers and Sellers?

Even though this isn't a training program, I have included enough of the "how" to get you started. Sections 8 and 10 contain the critical sales communications skills, forms, and scripts needed to ensure your success. Section 13 has the scripts and letters in its own section for you to practice and apply. If you're like lots of agents, you don't just want to read about it, you want to hear it.

The Four-Week Plan: This Is Your Life— Not Just Assignments

Even though I may call the activities in the four-week plan "assignments," they are not scholastic. They are business. You are starting your business with this business start-up plan. However, you can't do and learn everything at once. That's why I've allocated certain lead-generating activities to certain weeks, and certain business-supporting activities to certain weeks. At the end of the four weeks, I want you to be a salesperson "in the swing of things" who has contacted hundreds of people. I want you to be "packaged" and "practiced" so you are gaining skill with people and enjoying more success from your lead generating.

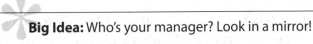

Big Idea: Who's your manager? Look in a mirror!

■ Managing "You"

There are two parts to managing your *Up and Running* program:

1. Managing the activities in the program
2. Managing your attitude during the program

Guess who manages these two parts: you do. You are in business for yourself, with your office and manager supporting you. This program is *driven* by you. If you want to capture the support of your manager, meet with him or her weekly. Go over your accomplishments in your business plan. In order to progress faster, get help in your support areas.

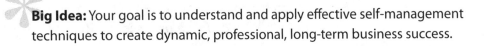

Big Idea: Your goal is to understand and apply effective self-management techniques to create dynamic, professional, long-term business success.

■ Getting Help from Your Manager

It's tough out there. Agents enter the real estate business with enthusiasm, hope, and determination. Then they find out what rejection means, and their enthusiasm quickly withers under the stress of starting anew.

Managers can help. This resource offers new agents (and those attempting to re-jump-start their careers) a game plan that will ensure a successful career. However, to start and continue a challenging program (whether it's a diet or a new job), every person needs encouragement—not just "atta boy, keep going" kind of support but *real, specific, constructive guidance and feedback* that will help the agent build a successful daily plan and know that it is working.

Managers Can Provide Emotional Support and Coaching Focus

In the quest to make a profit, managers must do everything from counsel agents to run the administrative part of the office. It's difficult for managers to provide new agents the guidance needed to get their careers off to a quick, successful start. *Up and Running* relieves managers' concerns because it provides the plan and resources new agents need to begin a successful career.

Big Idea: Managers *support* an agent's business; agents *drive* it themselves—with their managers as coaches.

Agents are responsible for completing each weekly plan. Managers who want to provide the highest level of support will meet with the agent weekly (the agent sets the appointment) to review the agent's accomplishments, provide encouragement, and add their expertise to the actions the agent is taking. The weekly checklists entitled "Your Start-Up Plan and Accomplishments" for Sections 4 through 7 have been created for just that use and are in Section 12.)

Armed with the *Up and Running* game plan, the weekly accomplishments, plus the other measurement tools, manager and agent can partner for the agent's quick success. (For a manager's coaching resource to partner with *Up and Running,* see the References section.)

Manager–Agent "Success" Agreement

As in any successful partnership, the new agent has the best chance to succeed when the agent and manager work closely together. To ensure that the manager and agent are sharing mutual expectations, use the Agreement to Ensure You're *Up and Running* (see Figure 3.2). Not only does your manager need to know your level of commitment, you want to know your manager's level of commitment, too.

Manager's Tip: Use this agreement during the interview process to ensure you and the agent have mutual expectations.

Aggressively Demanding Your Manager's Attention Is a Good Thing

If your manager doesn't come forward to ask to coach you, go to him or her! As a manager, I have come to recognize common success traits in agents. One distinguishing quality is the ability to demand a manager's assistance. Inversely, agents who hang back, afraid to ask for the manager's guidance, will be less successful. I really appreciate new agents who consistently make appointments with me to let me know what they are

---

FIGURE 3.2   Agreement to Ensure You're *Up and Running*

I, _____ , agree to complete all the assignments in the *Up and Running in 30 Days* start-up plan. I understand each aspect of the plan, and that it is constructed to help me get a fast start.

I want support from my manager, so I agree to make an appointment with my manager weekly. During that appointment, I will review the work completed for that week and my plan for the next week. I agree to:

1. Keep each appointment

2. Be on time

3. Be prepared

To ensure that I get the most from my plan, I expect my manager to:

- Meet with me weekly for at least one-half hour

- Help me keep my activities prioritized correctly

- Provide assistance in my development of specific business methods

- Provide me any resources necessary to complete the assignments

- Provide the support and encouragement necessary to begin a successful career

I understand it's my business, and I agree to manage it according to the principles in *Up and Running in 30 Days*.

Agent _____   Manager _____

Date of this agreement: _____   End of program: _____

---

doing, how they are doing it, and how I can assist them. That's called *managing the manager!* Obviously, these new agents get much of my attention, concern, and positive strokes—the fuel for motivation.

How to Get the Best from Your Manager

New agents want all the support they can get. Sometimes, though, they don't realize they may inadvertently be acting in a way that doesn't get the best from their managers. Their actions are training their managers to react to them differently than the agents really want their managers to act. For example, if you only come into the manager's office when you have a gripe, you are training your manager to run the other way when she sees your frowning face! If you don't take part in your team's activities, don't attend office meetings, and only appear when you want the manager's help, you are training that manager to believe you aren't a team player. If you don't get into action quickly, you're training your manager to think that her job is to constantly motivate you—not to support your action efforts. (And motivating someone who won't get into action becomes a very difficult and energy-expending job!)

Ten commandments. To assure you get the best from your manager, I've created ten commandments that ensure you will get the best from your manager. I don't mean your manager will play unfair favorites. I mean that your manager will get the cooperation and attitude she needs to *help you best*. Here are the commandments:

1. Do the work
2. Don't argue
3. Don't make excuses
4. Don't tell the manager you've been in the business two weeks and you have a better way
5. Do thank your manager
6. Do tell other agents that you appreciate your manager's efforts
7. Do tell other new agents you meet in other companies that you have a great manager
8. Don't bug other people in the office to find another answer because you didn't like your manager's answer
9. Don't change the program because you don't like it
10. Don't miss a coaching appointment

■ Should You Find an In-Office Coach?

Coaching fills the gap between the training room and real life. You may be able to find someone in your office or company who's willing to coach you if your manager is unable to do so. A good in-company coach can do the following:

1. Hold you accountable to the goals you say you want to accomplish
2. Share how-tos and packaging (such as listing packages)
3. Let you shadow her on a listing or buyer presentation or sales negotiation
4. Accompany you on presentations or sales negotiations

5. Remind you if you're off track—tell you the truth because your goals are important to you

6. Use good coaching skills

However, don't expect a coach to be an "answer man." And moreover, don't expect a coach to coach you if you don't have a specific game plan—such as the *Up and Running* start-up plan.

Big Idea: In-office coaching doesn't work unless the coach is trained and committed to you—and you're committed to your game plan.

Why Would Someone Want to Coach You?

You should be able to answer that question. And the answer isn't because you need lots of help! It's not all about you. Ask yourself, "What's in it for the coach?" (Heads up: Attaching benefits to features is an important sales skill you'll be learning. See Section 10.)

My opinion: You should *expect to pay your coach.* You should expect to sign a mutual expectations agreement. You should also expect that, if you don't follow your plan, your coach will fire you.

If coaching fails, it's usually because of three reasons:

1. The coach and agent had different expectations of each other. The contract needs to spell out exactly what is expected of each party.

2. The coach and agent didn't agree upon a game plan. If you want a coach, be prepared to get into action fast so the coach has something to coach you to! Don't expect your coach to motivate you to do the activities you know you should do—but won't!

3. The coach wasn't trained. Before you sign up with a coach, see the whole coaching program—in writing—to ensure it's really a program, not just an afterthought.

■ Watch Out Now for Dependent Tendencies

As you start your real estate career, it's inevitable that you will be feeling insecure of your abilities to sell real estate. All of us have felt that way. It's at this time you may start feeling "dependent"—your company owes you something. That something is probably a lead. Remember, however, leads aren't free. They cost money in terms of either commission splits or referral fees. You make the choice. Either you can work an aggressive lead-generating plan like *Up and Running in 30 Days,* or you can sit and wait for leads (and take the control for your success out of your hands). When you are wondering if you are starting your business correctly, read this—again.

Big Idea: Successful salespeople generate their own leads because they want to control their destinies.

■ Managing Your Attitude

We've talked about your managing your *Up and Running* plan. That's the "hard side" of the business—the facts, figures, and activities. However, there's something else you must manage: the "soft side" of the business—your attitude.

How Our Attitudes Change with the Challenge

One of the things we managers love about a new agent is the enthusiasm with which they start. You're excited to jump into sales. Sometimes you're even overconfident. You tell us managers you are tenacious and that you can handle rejection. You describe yourself as a self-starter; you assure us you can motivate yourself. Then, reality takes over. You've always thought of yourself as a good communicator. However, as you lead generate, you find it difficult to convince people to work with you. People somehow create many ways to reject you. You've always liked people, and you sense they like you. Yet they act differently with you now that you're in sales. People make up stories to avoid you, say they "have a friend in the business," secure information from you but do not give you information, promise to meet with you at the office—but don't show up. You experience these feelings:

- Rejection
- Frustration
- Impatience
- Self-doubt
- Inadequacy

Your image of yourself is tested. Who is the real *you?* The one who feels confident and tenacious and is a self-starter? Or the one who feels rejected, frustrated, inadequate, and full of self-doubt? Your attitude about the business—and yourself—is in danger of shifting from *positive* to *negative.*

Big Idea: The best way to change your attitude from negative to positive is to get a sale.

Attitudes can change in seconds. Each day, hour, and minute, you evaluate your feelings about the business. Your *experiences* as you perform the activities in this plan fuel this evaluation. Your *conclusions* are based on your personal belief system. It's not the activities that cause you to have a certain attitude about the business, but the conclusions you draw from your experiences with these activities. Let's say you have knocked on 50 doors without getting a lead. What do you conclude? Agents who will fail conclude that "this won't work in this area." Agents who will succeed imagine themselves one step closer to a lead with every rejection. These agents realize that they must experience many rejections to get success.

Big Idea: Tenacity is the one character attribute that is 99 percent of an agent's success.

Big Idea: Agents expect a sale in the first month. Not getting one puts their attitude in the dumper. Protection plan against an "in the dumper attitude": go out and talk to lots of people—fast.

Managing attitude shifts. Managers can teach new agents what activities to do, how to do them, and how to monitor them to evaluate effectiveness. Using the forms provided in this book, managers and agents can track agents' actual *behaviors* each day. But who will keep track of changing

FIGURE 3.3   Managing Attitudes

attitudes? Who will manage the conclusions about these activities? These emotional evaluations flit through a new agent's head hundreds of times a day. *How* these constantly changing attitudes are managed determines whether the agent will succeed.

What agents want. According to a recent survey of real estate salespeople, one of the most important services agents want from their manager is to *provide positive motivation.* Sounds easy, doesn't it? Part of it is. It's not difficult to create a positive atmosphere in the office. It is difficult to find out what motivates each individual (everyone has different motivators). And it is more difficult to design a motivational program to fit each agent's needs—time in the business, motivators, outside influences, and so on. Moreover, it's *very* difficult for a manager to manage the constant flux of attitudes to catch agents when they are falling into depression and to pump them up. Agents' attitudes change hundreds of times a day. When agents get down, they usually talk to themselves—negatively. How can managers manage agents' ups and downs? They can't—but they can teach new agents how to manage their ups and downs.

Recognize →
Acknowledge →
Develop New Conclusions

Becoming a managing master of your attitudes. Managing your attitude requires three steps:

1. *Recognize your attitude* about the business will change as you do the activities in the business.
2. *Acknowledge* each time you draw a conclusion about your activities.
3. *Develop a process* for drawing a positive, motivating conclusion.

Make an attitude notebook. To evaluate and manage your attitude, try this simple, effective method. In a notebook, divide each page into six columns:

1. Self-talk
2. Conclusions of your self-talk
3. Positive attitude
4. Negative attitude
5. Revised conclusion/revised attitude
6. Belief

As you go about your business day, keep your attitude notebook handy. Write down each time you talk to yourself—positively and negatively. Let's say you just held an open house. As you are leaving, you say to yourself: "What's wrong with me? I thought I was a good communicator, but these people coming into my open house won't tell me anything." Write down the conclusion you drew: "*Maybe I'm not cut out for this business.*" Note these thoughts in the proper column—*positive* or *negative.* Obviously, the above comment and conclusion would go in the negative column.

TABLE 3.1   Attitude Notebook Excerpts

Negative Self-Talk	**Positive Self-Talk**
I can't do this.	I learned a lot from this one.
I'm not cut out for this.	One down, one to go.
Why did they do that to me?	I'm getting better every day.
What's wrong with them?	I'm learning what I need to learn to succeed.

Drawing a positive, motivating conclusion. Studies show that most self-talk is *negative*, which naturally leads to a *negative* conclusion. People will talk to themselves about this conclusion 10 to 20 times and convince themselves that this conclusion is true! Thus, when agents conclude that they cannot be successful in open houses, that idea plays again and again in their minds until they change their positive attitude about their success in the business—and form a new belief about their ability to communicate.

You can stop this insidious—although natural—process by replacing it with a new process. To do this, you must replace your natural inclination of *negative* self-talk, repeated again and again, with some *positive* self-talk, repeated again and again.

Retraining your brain. Is this the conclusion about open houses that you really want to draw? Is this the attitude that will ensure your success in this business? Can you change your conclusion and attitude? Tough-minded, success-oriented people can adjust their conclusions and attitudes about their experiences to reach their goals. They experience the same rejection, self-doubt, frustration, and anxieties that failure-oriented people do. The only difference is that these tough-minded people have developed a mental system to reinterpret their conclusions. It's as simple as substituting a different conclusion, along with a change in attitude. So, go back to your attitude notebook and write a new conclusion to your experience. For the example above, it might be: *Based on my results, I'm not as good a communicator as I thought I was. I need to improve my communication skills. I can get these skills by taking a sales skills course, by observing agents who are successful at open houses, and by practicing my new skills.*

Big Idea: Tough-minded people train their brains to draw the best conclusions for their success.

Making your new conclusion believable. The last column in your attitude notebook, belief, is very important. If you don't believe that you can create a new conclusion, you will not take the action steps. In the belief column, add a statement that backs up your opinion about skills enhancement. It might be: *I know that, if other agents can be successful getting appointments at open houses, I can be, too. It's just a matter of my learning, practicing, and perfecting the skills required.*

Being tough-minded enough to succeed. The ability to *consciously* control your attitude is a skill that can be learned. To ensure your success in real estate, assume that you need to develop tough-mindedness. By following the steps outlined, you can become tough-minded enough to succeed in real estate.

There are many excellent self-help books on how to create a positive mental attitude, as well as courses and videos on self-esteem. One of the best courses, developed by Lou Tice, is offered at his Pacific Institute in Seattle, Washington.

Controlling your attitude is simple if you recognize that it's a *skill* that can be learned. It takes practice, tenacity, and patience. But isn't it worth it if it ensures your success in real estate? You have a proven, successful, activity-based, business-developing program in *Up and Running.* You have a manager committed to your success. You have the tools to retrain your mind and control your attitude. You are set for success!

 Big Idea: Start your *Up and Running* plan to get success fast; your attitude will take care of itself!

◼ *Up and Running:* An Overview of Your Four Weeks

You've gotten lots of advice on starting your career. You know how to manage your actions—and your attitudes. Now you're ready to start your four-week plan. Each week, for four weeks, you will complete the following activities:

1. *Create your weekly and daily plan.* Use the provided planners; refer back to the Prototype Schedule and *30 Days to Dollars* plan. Be sure to keep a balance of business-producing activities and business-supporting activities. Ask your manager to assess the balance of your plan. Creating your plan and assessing it, two of the most valuable

self-management tools in *Up and Running,* provide the basis for making good business judgments throughout your entire career.

2. *Complete the assigned activities in the* 30 Days to Dollars *lead-generating plan.* See each week of the four-week plan. It's all outlined for you. Use the provided spreadsheets to measure your results weekly.

3. *Complete your weekly schedule and daily plan* using the provided planners so you can stay on track daily and weekly.

4. *Practice and apply new sales skills.* New sales skills are assigned each week to prepare you for sales activities with buyers and sellers.

5. *Complete business-supporting activities,* such as preparing packages and presentations, evaluating buyers and sellers, implementing your marketing plan, and following up with buyers and sellers, to increase your confidence and help you manage your time better.

6. *Meet with your manager for support, information, and encouragement.* It's difficult to "go it alone," and your manager is committed to your success. *Up and Running* provides a solid foundation for communication between you and your manager.

■ Get Ready—Get Organized

I've provided a list of the materials you'll need to start your first week in the business in Figure 3.4 (there is a blank form for you to use in Section 12.) These include three three-ring notebooks, each at least one inch thick. You'll see how you're going to use them in week one, discussed in Section 4. So, your assignment prior to starting your week one is to do two things:

1. Finish your orientation with your manager and staff and complete all the actions requested of you (if you've already started or done your orientation). I've also assigned this in week one, because I don't know how long you've been in the business at this point.

2. Go through the Get Ready checklist in this section and gather all the materials you'll need. When you get the three-ring notebooks, name one attitude notebook, one office notebook, and one resource notebook. You'll see in Section 4 (week one) how you're going to use them.

Big Idea: Finish all the actions asked of you by your manager and staff within your first week of the business so you can launch your career with the support you need.

FIGURE 3.4   Get Ready: Gather the Tools of the Trade

Briefcase

Cell phone

Pen

Pencil

Colored pen or pencil

Calendar

Highlighter

Scratch pad

Post-it notes

Daily planner or PDA

Access to your MLS

Street map

Paper clips

Tape measure (100' or 30.5m)

Staple gun

Laptop computer

Hand-held calculator

Digital camera

Attitude notebook*

Office notebook*

Resource notebook*

Car

Sold signs

Tape

Mallet and nails

Screwdriver

Flashlight

Coveralls

Overshoes

First aid kit

Forms

Purchase and sale agreements

Wording for contract forms

Other contract addendas

Listing agreements

Other forms pertaining to listing

Other Materials

_____

_____

_____

*See "Get Ready—Get Organized"

Excerpted from *Advantage 2.0*, Carla Cross Seminars, Inc., 2005.

Manager's Tip: Be sure your orientation has an action plan of the items you expect agents to complete and a method to check off with them to ensure they've been accountable—quickly—to accomplish what you and your staff expect. This way, your agents get the support you promised during the interview, and they're ready to get to work.

■ **Summary**

Live each day as closely to that successful agent's job description as you can. Doing the *Up and Running* plan ensures that.

Your goal throughout this four-week plan is to develop the skills to self-manage your business. To do that, you need to

1. follow the *Up and Running* plan to the letter;
2. use the measurement spreadsheets and checklists I provided to help you self-manage;
3. rely on yourself, not on anyone else, including your manager, to hand you leads or keep you motivated;
4. manage your attitude with your attitude notebook—the best way to do that is to get out in the field *now* and go to work;
5. recognize you will underestimate your resilience to rejection and develop the mind skills to accentuate the positive and keep going; and
6. enlist your manager as your coach so you'll have an accountability partner.

Now, let's jump right into your week one start-up plan!

Week One Start-Up Plan

Let's start the first day of your successful career! Sections 4 through 7 are literally *your start-up plan.* In this section, you'll get the activity plan for your first week in the business. Also, because you're just starting this plan, I'll explain how to use the various tracking forms I've created. As you use these forms, you'll be developing exceptional time management skills. You don't know it yet, but time management is rated as the number one challenge agents have!

Throughout your four-week plan, you'll have a very detailed, precise weekly plan to follow.

Your activities are divided between

Business producing
and
Business supporting

They're divided and prioritized this way to train your mind to think like a top producer. Business-producing activities are involve directly finding and working with potential buyers and sellers. Business-supporting activities are those "get ready" and "practice" activities: packaging your presentations and processes, practicing your sales skills, and learning the technical aspects of the business.

■ Regular Activities Create Success Habits

Every week, you will have certain *regular* activities, so you'll develop automatic, unconscious success habits. Don't look for "new stuff" every week. What you need to do is to create the routine top producers use to generate and re-generate their businesses.

In the *business producing* category, every week you will

1. implement your *30 Days to Dollars* lead-generating plan by contacting at least 100 people using the methods introduced in that week,
2. get two qualified seller leads,
3. get two qualified buyer leads,
4. show homes to two qualified buyer groups, and
5. go to at least one listing appointment.

That number of business-producing activities ensures you are on the road to quick success. To make certain you are being accountable to your success, you will be setting goals in each of the areas above and measuring your successes.

Every week, you will have certain regular business-supporting activities to create the systems and processes you need to be trustworthy to buyers and sellers—and to raise your confidence.

Separating these activities into clear categories gives you focus. Doing these activities in sufficient numbers and in the right order creates success habits for you. These are the success habits of a top producer.

How Do I Do These Things?

There is a lot of training in this edition of *Up and Running*. In each week's activities, I have told you the time for that particular skill training. For example, in week one, you will be circle prospecting to get leads. The how-to is in Section 8. So don't worry that you'll have an action expected of you that you don't know how to do. Sections 8, 9, and 10 have all the how-tos, scripts, and forms you'll need. If there's additional training you want, ask your manager! In addition, your company training program may train you in sales skills and systems.

Scripts and Letters Section

Section 13 is new in this edition. It includes the scripts and letters introduced in this program so you can find them easily. These scripts and letters provide you the information you need to lead generate and master those critical sales skills.

Weekly Regular Business-Supporting Activities:

- Create your weekly schedule in advance of the following week
- Add at least 50 contacts to your database
- Write at least 15 follow-up notes
- Evaluate your buyers and sellers using the buyers and sellers evaluation sheets
- Work your marketing plan
- Work your technology plan
- Practice the sales skills assigned in week one
- Apply the sales skills that are assigned for week one in real life
- Add to your resource, attitude, and office notebooks
- Plan and measure your results: for the day-to-day measurements, use the Daily Planner; for week-to-week measurements, use the Weekly Accomplishments; also use the spreadsheets to compare your goals to your actuals (what you actually did)

 Manager's Tip: Increase your agents' knowledge base by creating an office resource book of helpful articles in lead generating and systems. You can find dozens of them in the publications you receive each week, and there are myriad articles online. This will provide additional support for your agents at little cost or time to you.

Organizing All the Information You'll be Getting

We've already talked about your attitude notebook, which you'll be writing in daily. Weekly, you'll see adding to it is a regular business-supporting assignment. In addition, there are two other notebooks I want you to create to organize all that information you'll be getting:

1. Office notebook
2. Resource notebook

I'll be reminding you weekly to add to them so you can find that valuable information you need—when you need it!

Why notebooks, not files? Because I want you to immediately see that notebook in a prominent place. I don't want you to agonize about what to call a file. I don't want you to file it away so you can't find it! I've tried it both ways, and a notebook is better. Also, some of these notebooks you'll want to carry with you.

Why not just keep these things in a computer folder? With some of them, you can. Make a folder called "Office Communication" and put all your office communication there. The challenge with that is you may forget to do it, put it in the wrong folder, and so on. I find that most people don't remember where they filed a document in their computer. Also, we're visual people, and we're tactile. Organizing hard copies of these things in notebooks means you have to look at them before you put them in your notebook. It means you look at them again naturally as you're searching for something in that notebook.

Big Idea: Use hard copy notebooks to start your career. They'll remind you of the many details you're bound to forget!

Office notebook. As you join your office, you'll be given all kinds of information about the office. You'll probably attend an office orientation. Where will you put all this information so you'll be able to find it when you need it? In your office notebook. This would include all the information you got from orientation, your office meeting agendas, phone system how-tos, anything you need to be able to locate later.

Resource notebook. Put all your information from your business-supporting activities in this notebook. For instance, when you talk with a loan officer, put all the information you got from her about interest rates, points, and so on to qualify a purchaser in this notebook. *Take the notebook with you in the field!* This will be a lifesaver for you when you're in an open house and a buyer asks, "What's the interest rate today?" Believe me, you will be getting so much valuable yet disparate information, you will not know what to do with it. Then, when you need it, you won't have it! So start your resource notebook today. You can make sections for these categories:

- Finance
- Inspections
- Title insurance
- Attorney's closing fees
- Escrow fees
- Home insurance
- Law updates
- New MLS rules

Keeping this information in a folder in your computer for reference is acceptable. But keep in mind that you won't look at it, compare it, delete it, or have it handy when you need it.

Definitions, definitions, definitions. One of the confusing things a new agent has to contend with is the many new terms thrown at him. For example, there's home insurance and mortgage insurance. What's the difference? You should have all those definitions in your resource notebook so you'll know—and be able to explain them to buyers and sellers. Don't always believe those seasoned agents when they explain things. They may not really know, either!

Big Idea: Start organizing now. *Any* organization is better than none.

■ Week One *Up and Running* Plan

These activities are all listed in your week one accomplishments document in Section 12 with the week one forms.

Business Producing

Implement your *30 Days to Dollars* lead-generating plan. Contact at least 100 people using these methods:

- Call or contact 50 people you know (see Section 8 for a script)
- Circle prospect 50 people (see Section 8 for definition and operation)
- Get two qualified seller leads
- Get two qualified buyer leads
- Show homes to two qualified buyer groups
- Go to at least one listing appointment

These assigned activities are already in your spreadsheets, your *30 Days to Dollars* lead-generating plan, and *30 Days to Dollars* lead-generating results for your week one in Section 12. All you need to do is to log in your actuals.

Business Supporting

Regular actions:

- Create your weekly schedule in advance of the following week (a blank form is in Section 12 for you, marked Week One)
- Add at least 50 contacts to your database
- Write at least 15 follow-up notes
- Evaluate your buyers and sellers using the buyers and sellers evaluation sheets (in Section 12)
- Do the activities in your marketing (follow-up) plan for that first week
- Practice the sales skills assigned in that particular week
- Apply the sales skills that are assigned for that week in real life
- Add to your resource notebook
- Add to your attitude notebook
- Add to your office notebook

At the end of the week, measure your results using the four measurements below. Before your appointment with your manager, do the following:

1. Daily, use the *Daily Planner*
2. Evaluate your time management on your *Weekly Schedule*
3. Check off your completed activities on your *Weekly Accomplishments*
4. Weekly, complete the *Goals/Actuals Spreadsheets*

Additional business supporting activities for your first week:

Sales skills:
- Using sales skill 1, craft a sales script to call on people you know (see Section 8)
- Using sales skill 3, ask for a lead (see Section 10)

- Create three visuals to counter seller's objections to pricing (see your manager or three agents in your office for suggestions; see Section 10 for training on answering objections)

Sales opportunities:

- If you're going to hold an open house or take floor time, get information from your manager on how to do each of these reactive lead-generating activities
- Observe two public open houses this weekend; interview the agents who hold them open about their methods
- Observe at least one hour of floor time this week (or, if you don't have floor time, observe three agents handling incoming calls)
- Interview the agents who take floor time about their methods

Technical information:

- Orientation: complete all your office orientation duties (get your business cards, etc.) and put all the information in your office notebook
- Meet with a loan officer and have that loan officer teach you the basics of financing (get a loan officer referral from your manager); put all that information in your resource notebook
- Ask three experienced agents to see their market analyses packages. Take notes so you can compile your own. Then, complete a market analysis on your own home. Practice presenting it to a "seller" so you'll be comfortable with the format and information.

Planning:

- Complete your real estate budget using the form called Budget for the New Agent in Section 12
- Make your technology plan using the Technology Planner in Section 12
- Create your marketing plan (see Section 9 for how to create your plan and a sample plan) using the Your Marketing Plan form in Section 12

■ Planning and Measuring Your Results

You know the importance of planning and measuring the plan. I've created the planning and measurement tools for you to make it easy for you to become a master at planning and measuring.

Every week, you will be using four methods to plan and measure your results:

1. *Your weekly schedule.* You'll set your schedule and evaluate it each week for effective time management.

2. *Your daily planner.* You'll use one page per day to self-manage effectively. At the end of the day, you'll evaluate the effectiveness of your day.

3. *Your weekly accomplishments.* You'll check off your assigned actions and do a self-evaluation for effective time management.

4. *Your goals/actuals spreadsheets.* You'll keep your completed business-producing actions on these spreadsheets so you can see your progress through time.

Section 12: All Your Blank Forms Ready to Use

To make it easy for you to use the forms, I've put them all in Section 12, with one set of forms for each week. Most of the forms are already filled out with that particular week's activities. All you have to do is to make any alterations you want to make (we hope you won't make any) and log in the actions you accomplished that week.

Why set your goals and track your accomplishments so frequently? Because you want to get into the habit. Most agents don't do this, and so have terrible time management problems.

How to Create Your Weekly Schedule

You have your start-up plan for your first week. Now, you need to make a weekly schedule that integrates the action steps in your plan. I've made a sample weekly schedule for you so you can see how your plan should look for its first week (see Figure 4.1).

Using the blank weekly planner for week one in Section 12, plan your first week. Create your plan in the following order:

1. Log in office-scheduled events (e.g., office meeting, tour)
2. Log in assignments from office (e.g., floor time, open house)
3. Log in your coaching meeting with the manager
4. Log in business-producing activities/those on business cycle (e.g., showings, listing presentations, writing offers)
5. Log in lead-generating activities
6. Log in support activities, including inspecting inventory and support assignments given here

Note: You may choose to enter your schedule into a personal digital assistant (PDA) or a pocket personal computer (PC). This will allow you to view your schedule at any time, along with your contacts and other pertinent information.

At the end of your week, evaluate how you did, using the evaluators in Your Weekly Schedule. Note the suggested hours weekly of various business-producing activities. How did you compare? Rate yourself on how effective

FIGURE 4.1   Sample *Up and Running* Weekly Schedule for Week One

Week: _____ One _____   Name: _____ Joan Smith _____

Time	Monday	Tuesday	Wednesday	Thursday	Friday	Saturday	Sunday
7–8	Organize desk		Day off	Write 40 follow-up cards			
8–9	Office meeting	Paperwork			Meet w/mgr	Paperwork	
9–10	Office tour	Call 20 people I know		Call 10 people to ask for leads	Call 20 people to ask for leads	Show homes	
10–11	→	→		→	→	→	Show homes
11–12	Lunch	Floor time		Paperwork	Inspect	Lunch	→ Lunch
12–1	Office orient.	Lunch		Lunch	Lunch	Floor time	Lunch
1–2	Inspect inventory	Start market analysis		Inspect inventory	Inspect	→	Follow-up
2–3	→	→		→	Bus. support work	Inspect inventory	In-person visits to five people
3–4	Call 20 people I know	Follow-up		Follow-up	→	→	
4–5	List 100 people to ask for leads	Inspect inventory		Meet with loan officer	Circle prospect 25 homes	Circle prospect 25 homes	→
5–6	→	→		→	→	→	
6–7							
7–8							Do listing presentation
8–9							→

Suggested Hours Weekly:

Lead generating	10
Qualifying buyers/sellers	5
Show properties/listing properties	5
Purchase/sale agreements	5

What You Did

_____ hours
_____ hours
_____ hours
_____ hours

How could you improve your schedule?

Evaluate Your Weekly Schedule
Rate yourself in the effectiveness of your weekly schedule: _____
1–10 (10 is high)

you believe that particular weekly schedule was for you. Now you're developing the time management tools other agents will envy!

Why Evaluation Is So Important for You

Unfortunately, most people think the first time they do something is as good as it's going to get! Why? Because they don't know how to get better at something. As a lifelong performing musician, I know you don't have to settle for mediocre performance. I know the first time I do something isn't as good as that performance will be later. I know how to get better. I've built evaluators into this program because it's one of the methods I use as a performance coach to increase my clients' confidence and help them get performance mastery.

Big Idea: Evaluating how you did automatically creates better performance next time.

■ How to Create Your Daily Plan

You've created your weekly schedule. Now, manage your actions daily by using the Daily Planner, shown in Figure 4.2. (Blank daily planners are included for each of the four weeks in Section 12. You will copy these so you have one for each day of the week.) Why do it daily? To ensure you are establishing top-flight time management habits! Also, by tracking your accomplishments daily, you'll be able to congratulate yourself as you go—and quickly make the needed adjustments in your plan.

How to Use the Week One (and Ensuing Weeks) Accomplishments

I've put all the actions in your start-up plan for each week into your weekly Accomplishments document. There is one for each week in Section 12. All you have to do is to complete the actions and log them in. Now, meet with your manager weekly to review your accomplishments and challenges.

How to Use the Goal/Actual Spreadsheets

Figures 2.6 and 2.7 are a concise way to look at your goals and accomplishments for each week through time. In Section 12, I have created a goal/actual spreadsheet entitled "Your *30 Days to Dollars* Lead-Generating Plan"

FIGURE 4.2 *Up and Running* Daily Planner

Date: _____

Priorities: **Accomplished**   **Notes:**

1. _____   ❑   _____

2. _____   ❑   _____

3. _____   ❑   _____

4. _____   ❑   _____

5. _____   ❑   _____

6. _____   ❑   _____

7. _____   ❑   _____

8. _____   ❑   _____

9. _____   ❑   _____

10. _____   ❑   _____

	Lead Generating	Qualified Leads	Listing Appointments	Home Showings
Activity				
Hours Spent				

	Listings Obtained	Sales	Listings Sold
Results			

Rate your efforts on a scale of 1–10 _____

How can you improve your rating? _____

_____

At the end of the week, transfer your numbers of activities to your spreadsheets in Section 12.

Note: Make six copies of this sheet per week.

with the assignments in your *Up and Running* plan. All you have to do is to log in your results. Take these tools with you when you meet with your manager, so you can see your progress over this four-week time frame.

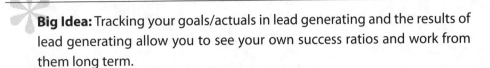

> **Big Idea:** Tracking your goals/actuals in lead generating and the results of lead generating allow you to see your own success ratios and work from them long term.

■ Final Thoughts for Week One

If you are like many new agents, at the end of week one your brain feels like mush. New words, new systems, unfamiliar territory—no wonder that new agents may reevaluate their charge-ahead attitude and decide to ease into the career! They reason that they must spend more time on learning, research, and organization—instead of talking to people so quickly. Their confidence decreases as rejection increases. New agents conclude that to increase their confidence they need more knowledge.

Build Real, Lasting Confidence

Up and Running is designed to build your confidence the right way—through increasing your skills. Real estate is a performance art, not a knowledge pursuit; true confidence in real estate is built from successful performance. However, until you perform, you have only your practice and imagination to build your confidence. Although there are methods to increase your confidence mentally, they pale before the reality of a great performance.

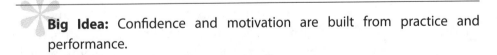

> **Big Idea:** Confidence and motivation are built from practice and performance.

The Value of Practice

It's painful to learn from your mistakes with real customers. However, there's an additional way to learn skills—practice. All too often, the value of practice is underestimated by both agents and managers. But it's worth the effort to role-play each segment that requires sales communication with people:

- Lead generating scenarios
- Counseling/qualifying buyer scenarios
- Showing and closing buyer scenarios
- Presenting and negotiating offer scenarios
- Qualifying seller scenarios
- Marketing/presentation scenarios
- Price reduction/review scenarios

Agents believe that because they can talk they can sell. But we have already discussed the realities of conversation versus the special communication skills required for sales success. I guarantee that if you take seriously the practice asked of you in *Up and Running,* your performance with people will improve quickly and your confidence will soar. Every successful salesperson I have known who started quickly in this business organized, systematized, practiced, and perfected each step in the sales cycle.

Caution: A reason new agents start slowly or fail early is that they underestimated their need to develop a mastery of sales skills in their first months in the business.

Perfect Practice Makes Perfect

The best kind of practice increases your skill and results. Back to my piano-practicing days: as a four-year-old, I picked out tunes on the keys and added the chords. I could play pop music reasonably well. Then, at age six, I started piano lessons. As I progressed to more demanding piano teachers, I learned that "faking it 'til you made it" just would not meet their standards. In fact, my best piano teacher, Mr. Green, taught me to practice very slowly, *so there weren't any mistakes.* I found that if I practiced quickly, I practiced my mistakes right along with the rest of the piece.

Although his kind of practice was tedious, it was right. By using Mr. Green's method I became a much better pianist, gaining a degree in piano performance. Too often, real estate agents practice the mistakes and end up with a sales system that is "more mistake than effective."

Big Idea: Perfect practice makes perfect. Go for mastery, not just mediocrity. One of a coach's opportunities is to help you "practice perfectly."

A Desire to Do It Again

If you have ever experienced the exhilaration of a fine performance, you know you want to run right out and do it again! Success is a great motivator. As we progress through Sections 4–7 we will be discussing self-motivation. For now, suffice it to say that good performance is the best motivator—and, correspondingly, the best motivator for selling is selling. This is the greatest reason to get out into the real estate field, even before you are comfortable: to motivate yourself to continue your quest for a successful real estate career.

■ Summary

Week one activities have you jumping right into your career. After all, you want to make a sale fast, so we're starting you fast! In week one, you are making a total of 100 sales calls. You're likely to get

- two qualified buyer leads and two qualified seller leads,
- two buyer showings, and
- one listing presentation.

What a start to your career!

This is also the week that you'll want to get all of that housekeeping out of the way. Organize everything. Learn the office operations. Find out how to do those reactive activities, like floor time, if you have it. Start learning the technical aspects of the business, like finance, as assigned in your business-supporting activities. We've also started you in skill development—learning and practicing those sales calls and sales skills that will get you more business easier. Finally, you started using the time-management tools that ensure you get started like a future superstar.

Congratulate yourself for an action-packed, focused first week in the business.

Week Two Start-Up Plan

Welcome to week two of your four-week start-up plan. This week you will learn and put into action additional types of lead generation—one of the priorities in your *30 Days to Dollars* lead-generating plan. They are:

- For-sale-by-owner or expired listings (you choose)
- Open houses

Even though you may choose not to use some of the lead-generating methods introduced here long term, you are expanding your skills. You are developing a lead-generating "repertoire," so you'll have it when you need it. When I was in college, I worked my way through school playing piano in bars. (I learned more about human nature than I really wanted to know!) I found that the more tunes and styles I could play, the more tips I made. Hence, I developed a wide repertoire. I never knew when it would come in handy. Having several lead-generating skills available to you is your insurance plan against changing markets.

■ Week Two *Up and Running* Plan

Besides learning more sales skills in week two, you will start assembling your systems for managing the buyer and seller sales processes. By the end of this program, I want you to have complete systems in place so you can go faster, build better, and create your business on the strongest foundation possible. Here are your actions for this week.

Business Producing

30 Days to Dollars: Make 100 sales contacts using these lead-generating methods:

- Make 25 contacts to people you know
- Circle prospect 50 people
- Call on at least 25 for-sale–by-owner or expired listings (see Sections 8 and 10 for skill development)

Reactive lead-generating action: hold one public open house this weekend. To prepare and develop the best strategies, talk to three people in your office. Even though I've assigned only one open house in this series, if you are encouraged to do this in your company, and you have traffic in these houses, assign yourself at least one open house per week.

Get these three results:

1. Secure two qualified buyer appointments
2. Show homes to two qualified buyer groups
3. Secure one appointment to do a listing presentation

These assigned activities are already in your spreadsheets, your *30 Days to Dollars* lead-generating plan, and your *30 Days to Dollars* lead-generating results for your week two (in Section 12). All you need to do is to log in your actuals.

Business Supporting

Do these regular actions:

- Create your weekly schedule in advance of the following week (a blank form is in Section 12 for you)
- Add at least 50 contacts to your database
- Write at least 15 follow-up notes
- Evaluate your buyers and sellers using the buyers and sellers evaluation sheets (in Section 12)
- Do the activities in your marketing (follow-up) plan for this week
- Practice the sales skills assigned in this week
- Apply the sales skills that are assigned for this week in real life
- Follow your Technology Planner
- Add to your resource notebook
- Add to your attitude notebook
- Add to your office notebook

At the end of the week, measure your results using the four measurements below. Before your appointment with your manager,

---

FIGURE 5.1   Suggestions for Seller Presentations

Materials can include:

1. How you publicize the property to other agents (show a list of agents and an example of an e-mail you send them)
2. How you advertise the property (show examples of your company advertising
3. How you make a brochure for the property (show a sample of the brochure/flyer you use)
4. How you publicize the property on company/your Web site (show a picture of one of your listings on the Web site and how you publicize it)
5. How you hold open houses (show a checklist of what you do to prepare for the open house; show pictures of you holding the home open)
6. Your checklist for after the listing is signed (to prove that you are organized and responsible)
7. What services your company provides (list all the services, and why they are important to the seller)
8. The services you provide (such as circle prospecting, contacting other agents, etc.)
9. The differences about your company (list them)
10. How you are different as an agent (list and show them)
11. Pricing principles (and why overpricing is not in the seller's best interest)
12. Market trends
13. Marketing plan (in writing)
14. Marketing calendar (in writing)
15. Pictures of homes you've listed/sold
16. Testimonials of those you have worked with (should also be in your professional portfolio)

Excerpted from *Your Client-Based Marketing System*, Carla Cross Seminars, Inc.

---

1. use the Daily Planner,
2. evaluate your time management on your weekly schedule,
3. check off your completed activities on your weekly accomplishments, and
4. complete the *goals/actuals spreadsheets* weekly.

Additional business-supporting assignments include the following:

- *To master sales skills:* Practice and apply sales skill #4, Objection-Busting (see Section 10)
- *Listing presentation:* Start assembling listing presentation materials (talk to your manager for ideas and a possible company presentation, and see the References section)
- *Assembling your listing presentation:* To assemble your materials, put into a folder the information you want to share with sellers about your services. Figure 5.1 gives you suggestions about what can go into this presentation.

After you have chosen the materials you want to include, put them in an order that makes it easy for you to present them. Sales tip: as you assemble the materials, ask yourself, "Which objection does this particular visual counter?" See more about visuals to handle objections in Section 10.

Review three agents' listing presentations and take notes. Integrate their ideas, with their permission, into your marketing presentation.

Interview three agents on the three most common objections sellers have to listing, and how these agents handle these objections. Write their answers and practice the ones you like best.

Buyer presentation. Assemble a buyer presentation, similar to a seller presentation but focused for buyers (see your manager and the References section for ideas). Figure 5.2 also gives you ideas about what you can put into a buyer presentation.

Review three agents' buyer presentations and take notes. Integrate the ideas you like, with their permission, into your buyer presentation. By the way, you may find that few agents in your office use buyer presentations. However, with the majority of buyers being represented by buyer's agents, it's very important to treat buyers as though they are as important as sellers—because they are!

FIGURE 5.2   Suggestions for Buyer Presentations

Materials can include:

1. The steps in purchasing a home
2. Time line for purchasing a home
3. Steps after you've purchased the home
4. Loan application checklist
5. Home inspection checklist
6. Offer preparation checklist
7. The parties involved in the purchasing process—and what they do
8. Market conditions
9. Describe your ideal home
10. Prioritize your home needs
11. How I work for you
12. How to choose the right agency relationship for you
13. Types of agency representation
14. Services of a buyer's agent
15. The buyer's agency agreement
16. Checklist for the buying experience
17. Advice to buyers
18. What is a REALTOR®?
19. Most used terms
20. If we work together
21. My commitment to you

Excerpted from *The Complete Buyer's Agent Toolkit*, Carla Cross Seminars, Inc.

Interview three agents about the three most common objections buyers have to buying and how these agents handle these objections. Write their answers and practice the ones you think are best.

To gain technical skills. Write two purchase and sale agreements. Include one practice agreement for purchasing the property you currently own, and one using a method to purchase other than conventional financing.

■ Why Put All That Time into Creating Visual Systems?

The Benefits of Visuals

- Builds credibility
- Is self-teaching
- Helps organize
- Counters objections
- Builds confidence

This week, I've asked you to start organizing your seller and buyer visual presentations. Why? Because I want to give you every bit of support, every bit of guidance, every bit of added edge I can to ensure you convert leads to customers and clients. Creating visual systems does five things for you:

1. It makes you look credible and professional—we believe what we *see,* not what we hear.
2. It is a self-teaching tool—you'll learn how to counter those objections and how to present to buyers and sellers 100 percent faster with these tools than without them.
3. You'll learn how to best organize your presentation to flow smoothly.
4. You'll learn the visuals that best counter the common objections.
5. It is a great confidence-building tool—you will never feel like you're out on a limb without the answers to sellers' and buyers' questions.

Trying to give a professional presentation without the visuals is like trying to play a Mozart sonata just by listening to it. Trust me. It can't be done. Not only is it very difficult to remember what you wanted to say to a buyer or seller when you're under stress, it just isn't nearly effective for you. I know because I've had agents do listing presentations in class for other agents with visuals and without them. The agents without visuals were voted worse presenters and not as credible as those with visuals!

You're Going to See and Hear the Good, the Bad, and the Ugly

When you talk to agents in your office about presentations and objections, you are going to be amazed. Some of the information you get will be very good. Some will be very outdated. Some will be outright wrong or bad. What may be stunning to you is the lack of substantiation for what agents tell you. Even though we've been teaching agents for years to "put your visuals where your mouth is," most agents just think they can talk people into anything!

Big Idea: Put your visuals where your mouth is.

Tell the truth attractively. We all know that overpriced listings don't sell. That's the truth. But when we tell sellers their overpriced listing won't sell, sellers just think we want a quick commission! So, we need to tell the truth "attractively." To do that, we need to show third-party endorsement. That is, we need to show the statistics credible organizations like the National Association of REALTORS® (see References) and our multiple listing services provide us. We need to show articles on market trends and reports on these trends by survey agencies. That way, we don't sound like we're just selfish salespeople. Instead, it's clear that we know what we're talking about because we're substantiating it with credible information. Start thinking like that now, and you'll gain the trust and loyalty of many more buyers and sellers than you would by just talking!

Big Idea: Working hard now to provide credibility and substantiation for your claims gains you loyal customers and clients—for life.

Big Idea: Trust isn't gained by buffaloing someone. It's gained by telling the truth attractively, by keeping your promises, and by putting the client ahead of yourself.

■ Stop Before You List That Property!

Here's some training advice. This advice is very blunt, because you are going to see lots of practices and get some advice that are not in the best interest of sellers and buyers. And, because you're new, you're going to be confused about what are really "best practices." So, forgive my bluntness, but I feel that's what it takes here! I'm putting this in week two because you may already have a lead to list a property by this point. If you're like most new agents, you think any listing is better than none. After all, it's something to practice on. At least, that's what I thought. But as I gained a few more months in the business, I realized how listing overpriced properties hurt everyone—the seller, the office, and me. So don't list it yet. Before you do, ask yourself the following questions:

1. Is this listing going to sell within normal market time? If not, why it is in a seller's best interest that I list this property? (Studies show that listings that don't sell quickly end up staying on the market much longer, and ultimately sell for less than they are worth—the old shopworn principle.)
2. Am listing this property just to get a listing? (If so, in my opinion, you're not practicing seller agency, you're practicing "agent agency." You just want sign and ad calls, or maybe you want to impress your broker.)
3. Is this listing going to make a better reputation for me, or a worse one? (If it doesn't sell, you will get a poor reputation both with homeowners and other agents.)
4. Is this listing consistent with my values? (Do you feel that you put the best interest of the client first, or are you putting your best interests first?)

The simple reasons we list overpriced properties are that we

1. want a listing so we can use it to snag ad and sign calls or impress our broker,
2. don't know what to say to a seller to get it priced right, and
3. don't realize we're costing the seller thousands of dollars and are adversely affecting the reputations of our office, other agents, and ourselves.

You'll find agents in your area (or even in your office) whose strategy is to "list everything." I caution you against that strategy for the reasons above. I believe that listing properties that won't sell in normal market time is mostly the cause of the poor reputation we have earned with consumers. You can be a part of changing that reputation, or you can confirm it!

Big Idea: Listing overpriced properties is not a service to your office, your associates, the seller, or you.

Resources to Set Standards of Practice

In Section 9, I've given you four documents with which you can set your standards of practice for sellers and buyers. That way, you're not wasting your time or misleading your customers and clients. These are exceptional time-management tools. In addition, they will help you hold to the standards you said you wanted to practice *before* you went into this business. Remember, buyers and sellers are looking for that agent who will tell them the truth—in their best interests!

Big Idea: There are many ways to practice real estate. The really successful agents practice it in the best interests of sellers and buyers.

■ Final Thoughts for Week Two

If you have been lead generating consistently, you have probably found some buyers to qualify. It's hoped that you have even shown houses to a few buyers this week. On the listing side, you have found at least one homeowner who was interested in selling his or her home. You have made one listing presentation. As the list grows and opportunities increase, you begin to experience some time management challenges. To help you manage your time, try the following recommended solutions.

Continue Your Weekly Plan

It's amazing how many agents don't plan their week *ahead* of their week! In fact, from teaching sales skills workshops, I have found that less than 10 percent of experienced agents actually lay out a week's work in advance. When they look at what they have accomplished the prior month, they are stunned. From analyzing their prior month's activities, they discover that they have been nonproductive because they

- let non-income-producing activities dominate their schedule,
- allowed well-meaning people to steal their time, and
- placed too much emphasis on support activities.

They became their own assistants! However, with new insights, agents can get back on track and create a plan that helps them reach their goals. *Up and Running* teaches you, from the beginning, how to prioritize your activities so that you can avoid this common mistake. Take advantage of your manager's help in staying focused and on track.

Don't Stop Lead Generating

The good news is you are getting some results from your lead generating. The bad news is that you will be tempted to stop lead generating. After all, it's more fun working with people than finding them! However, your income directly depends on your lead-generating numbers. It isn't true that we can *ever,* no matter how long we're in the business, stop lead generating. Says my friend Bill Feldman, former real estate agent, owner, and head of business development for one of the largest regional companies in the United States, "When you stop pedaling the bicycle, you fall off." Pedaling the bicycle fast enough to stay on track simply means planning, executing, and measuring your business start-up plan to provide you with enough new leads to get the results that will meet your goals.

Big Idea: The best experienced agents *never* stop lead generating because they know it's the cornerstone of a productive business.

Are You Resisting Getting into Action?

I'll bet you didn't know how challenging real estate sales were until now. To cope with those challenges, your creative subconscious may be coming up with ways to convince you to avoid getting into action. You might even start believing your subconscious! One of the most common reasons is the old "I can't do that because I don't know enough." Or, maybe your subconscious has convinced you that you're not organized enough to get into action, or that you're not perfect enough.

Ned, an agent in my office, acted in a way that is an example of creative avoidance. In the business eight months, Ned had made only one sale. However, he was in the office regularly and appeared busy with paperwork. He attended law courses and was well-informed on financing. One day I saw Ned collating maps. I asked him what he was doing. He explained that he was putting together a series of maps for a buyer's tour. I thought that was exceptional; buyers would really want to know the whereabouts of the homes they were seeing. Unfortunately, Ned had used his strategy with only six buyers—all the buyers he had put in his car in the past eight months! He had spent his time on this nifty map system, but had not talked to enough people to get them into the car—or have the opportunity to appreciate the map system! Which is more important to your goal attainment—talking to people, qualifying them, and showing them homes, or working diligently on a map system in case you find someone who wants you to show them homes?

How do you "get into action"? In a wonderful book, *The Conative Connection*, Kathy Kolbe explores the ways different personalities get into action—not how we learn, but how we get into action. Some people barge ahead and worry about the details later. We start badly, but, because we're tenacious, we surprise people by how good we finally get. Unfortunately, our supervisors often remember only how bad we were when we started. We must be tough-minded and keep at it; we must retain an image of ourselves as "finished products," because others will not see us that way. Other people observe the action for a long time. Finally, when we feel ready to perform well, we get into action. We start slowly but well. Because of our slow start, we don't get much positive reinforcement from our supervisors (or coach or manager), who note our lack of progress compared with others in the office. If slow starters are tenacious and believe in themselves, they become very good because they practice perfectly. Kolbe points out several "get into action" styles. This book will help you pinpoint your "get into action" style as well as the barriers and challenges you face as you start your real estate career.

Go ahead—be embarrassed. There is no way to be experienced until you get experience. No agents like to take risks, be embarrassed, or have buyers and sellers guess that they are new in the business. But face it—everyone has been new in the business. Just go ahead and get those first few months over with. You will be embarrassed every day—many times. As a new agent, my most common statement to buyers or sellers was "I don't know, but I'll find out." In music, little could stump me—but in real estate *anything* could stump me! Still, I muddled through it, and you will, too.

Big Idea: Your ability to get into action and risk being embarrassed is one of the attributes of a successful new agent.

Why not take your time? I've interviewed prospective agents who told me they really didn't want to sell real estate right away. They wanted to learn everything they could. Then, after six or eight months, they would feel ready to sell real estate. It doesn't work that way! I wish I could tell you that you can successfully launch your real estate career by taking lots of time to "get ready." However, if you take all the time in the world, you will fail for three reasons:

1. *Real estate is a performance art.* It doesn't matter how much you know; it only matters how you interact with people. And that takes practice and performance. To remember and emulate good performance, we need to perform right after we have heard, seen, and practiced that performance. Learning something in a class and letting that skill lie dormant for months just guarantees poor skill—and high stress.

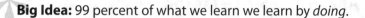

Big Idea: 99 percent of what we learn we learn by *doing*.

2. *The only true motivator is a sale.* Tell me you're in no hurry, that you have plenty of time to make your first sale. Tell me you're not concerned that you make a sale fast. I predict within three months, you'll be mentally and emotionally out of real estate. Why? Because you'll see others around you making sales and getting listings. The agents in the office will be congratulating them. You'll feel left out. Good agents in the office won't spend time with you, and you won't know why. After all, you have lots of questions you need answered, and you believe they should answer them. (I've never figured out why a new agent would think it's an experienced agent's duty to be an "answer man.") You'll find it's tough to stay motivated without some positive reinforcement. The longer it takes you to make a sale, the more reasons you will find to leave the business.

Big Idea: If you want to motivate yourself, make a sale.

3. *Your manager and/or coach and/or experienced agents will lose interest in you.* Because they don't see you taking meaningful action steps, your mentors will naturally become less motivated to help you. For you to stay motivated, you need the positive support of your mentors. From my experience, it takes about two months for managers and mentors to lose interest in a new agent. If an agent doesn't go to work fast, I, as a manager, may feel as if I've failed. No matter how motivating I've tried to be, nothing seems to be working. I feel like I'm expending a lot of energy for nothing. Then, I turn my attention to other agents who are creating activities. It not only makes me feel better, but it makes me feel as though my program works! (It also makes me feel appreciated. After all, we managers are human!) It's difficult and time-consuming to constantly think of new ways to motivate agents—over and over—after they are deflated!

Big Idea: It's your job to motivate yourself. It's your manager's job to hold you accountable to the plan and appreciate your efforts. Cause your manager/coach/agents to stay interested in you by taking the actions in *Up and Running* every day.

■ Straight Ahead and Strive for Tone

A drummer I worked with used to tell me this as I hesitated on the stand about launching into a challenging jazz piece. I'd start to chicken out, and Doug would yell, "Straight ahead and strive for tone!" What that means is, quit agonizing and theorizing about it, and just do it! Do it the best you can—and you'll learn how to do it better. You'll also surprise yourself once in awhile about how well you did. That will motivate you to do it again.

■ Summary

Congratulations! You've just contacted 100 more people; you've gotten some sales results from your efforts. You've continued honing your sales skills and sales packaging. You're starting to systematize your work with buyers and sellers. You're substantiating your claims with visuals. You're creating trust and confidence for long-term results and lifelong loyalty. You're on your way to a career that will truly be a business, not just an avocation! Now, on to week three.

Week Three Start-Up Plan

This week you will add to your lead-generating and sales skill repertoire. To gain confidence in purchase and sale agreements, you will write some agreements using different methods of financing. To increase your credibility with buyers and sellers, make these exercises challenging.

Even though you are new in the business, now is the time to set yourself apart from the crowd, and you will have an exercise in this week's action plan to do just that.

■ Time to Assess Your Progress

Now you have enough lead-generating numbers to analyze your results and make adjustments. You'll see, in your week three plan, that you'll be asked to look at your numbers. Ask yourself these two questions:

1. What are my best sources of leads so far?
2. Am I getting the number of appointments I need to attain my goals?

If you're not getting the number of appointments you need to get sales and listings, *increase your number of best lead-generating activities.* Now you're in the world of self-management.

■ Week Three *Up and Running* Plan

These activities are all listed in your week three accomplishments in Section 12, Week Three forms.

Business Producing

30 Days to Dollars: Make 100 sales contacts using these lead-generating methods:

- Make 25 calls to people you know
- Circle prospect 25 people
- Choose from other methods for another 50 proactive contacts
- Hold one open house

Get these results:

- Secure two qualified buyer appointments
- Show homes to two qualified buyer groups
- Secure one appointment to do a listing presentation
- List one marketable property

Time to stop and assess your ratios of lead generation to results. If you are not getting enough appointments, increase your lead generating. These assigned activities are already in your spreadsheets, your *30 Days to Dollars* lead-generating plan, and your *30 Days to Dollars* lead-generating results for week three (in Section 12). All you need to do is to log in your actuals.

Business Supporting

Do these regular actions:

- Create your weekly schedule in advance of the following week (a blank form is in Section 12 for you)
- Add at least 50 contacts to your database
- Write at least 15 follow-up notes
- Evaluate your buyers and sellers using the buyers and sellers evaluation sheets (in Section 12)
- Do the activities in your marketing (follow-up) plan for this week
- Practice the sales skills assigned in this week
- Apply the sales skills in real life that are assigned for this week
- Follow your Technology Planner
- Add to your resource notebook
- Add to your attitude notebook
- Add to your office notebook

At the end of the week, measure your results using the four measurements below. Before your appointment with your manager,

1. use the daily planner,
2. evaluate your time management on your weekly schedule,

3. check off your completed activities on your weekly accomplishments, and

4. complete the goals/actuals spreadsheets weekly.

Additional business-supporting assignments include the following:

To master sales skills:

- Practice and apply sales skill #5, the hum technique (see Section 10)
- Gain performance excellence with sales skill #5 (see Section 10).
- Practice your listing presentation three times (see your manager for presentations or see the References section)
- Practice your buyer presentation three times (see your manager for presentations or see the References section)
- Gather three visuals to counter sellers' objections (see your manager or the References section)
- Gather three visuals to counter buyers' objections (see your manager or the References section)

To gain technical knowledge:

- Learn two methods of writing purchase and sale agreements using alternative methods of financing, including one offer contingent on the sale of the purchaser's home. See your manager for help with this.

To promote yourself and gain more business:

- Start gathering the information you need to create a professional portfolio. See Section 9 for more information.

■ Maintain That "Successful Agent" Job Description

You are learning good business habits that lead to creating a *productive* business. You are correctly prioritizing your activities in order to build the right job description. However, because you have many other "job description models" (agents who aren't productive) in your business, you may be tempted to drop your *Up and Running* plan. After all, it's not easy to complete all those lead-generating and business-supporting activities that fast!

Be careful who you model. John (not his real name) was an agent in the first office I managed. When I was still working as an agent, I admired John's depth of information about waterfront property. Everyone went to him to learn what waterfront listings were on the market at any given time. Since I never kept track of that information, I figured I would get it from him! John was happy to help me out. Later, when I became manager of the office, I discovered that John was completing only four transactions a year—in his third year in the business—not enough to continue to build his business or support our office image as full-time, committed professionals. Yet John, who had received positive reinforcement for his *knowledge*, was content. As we had established standards of excellence in our office (which included production minimums), it was my job as a manager to work with John to help him increase his production. Working together, John and I agreed that for him to stay with our office, he would have to change his job description from *waterfront expert* to *successful salesperson*. In fact, it proved impossible— John liked the comfort of collating and the importance accorded him as a "waterfront expert" more than the excitement of selling real estate.

Big Idea: Behavior that's rewarded is repeated.

■ Create the Future—Your Way

You have been in the business three weeks. Is your image of yourself different from the one you had when you started in this business? Successful performers have learned to create a completed picture of themselves as great performers—*long before they are terrific performers.* This helps them to predict the outcome of their efforts. If you don't know where you're going, you can't get there!

Lou Tice, the founder of Pacific Institute, calls this skill *self-efficacy.* It is the ability to create yourself as a finished product in your head and hold that image, even though no one in the outside world has a clue that you are going to end up that way. What a skill! This technique is practiced in karate. When our son, Chris, took karate lessons he first watched great performers—black belts—performing the *katas* (fighting moves in a format) and *kumite* (actual fighting). Then he envisioned himself performing each part of these moves— just like they did. Finally, he performed the moves for his coach, very slowly, *practicing perfectly.* His coach watched carefully to ensure that he was practicing perfectly. After he perfected each move in context, he practiced performing faster. This method of creating perfect performance paid off. He won many medals in national and international competition—even while experiencing great growth spurts. His developed skill of self-efficacy ensured that his mind would hold the picture of his perfect performance. This skill has proved to be invaluable throughout his life.

Big Idea: To become a master of whatever you want, hold your future picture of yourself more strongly than your present reality.

Develop the Professional "You"

Take a few minutes in a quiet place by yourself. Imagine yourself as the successful real estate agent you intend to be. What will you do? What kind of recognition and power will you gain? What affiliations will you make that reflect your ideal of yourself as a pro? Create a movie with you as the star, complete with the movement, color, dialogue, tastes, and smells. Make it fun, exciting, and rewarding—in color. Play it over and over in your head 20 times a day for a month. Doing this will counteract your "growth spurts"—objections, barriers, negative self-talk, lost leads—as you start your career. You must develop some *mental ammunition.* Remember, people treat you as they see you. They can't see the new movie you have created until you start acting it out. Even then, they will try to put you back into your "old movie." It's human nature. Unwittingly, we help our friends fail by not becoming supporting players in their new picture. You must have a strong movie to move yourself in the direction you want to go so that others can get caught up in the new action and let go of the old.

Big Idea: Develop an ideal future "movie" of yourself, with color, sound, and feeling.

Show That You're the Professional of Choice

Recently, an agent who had been in the business about a year told me she couldn't get people who came to her open houses to appreciate her belief that she could help them. The reason she couldn't get them to appreciate her was that she didn't have time to engage them in conversation—to show them that she was knowledgeable and caring. Before she could talk to them, they were inching out the door. Her problem, stated in context of self-efficacy, was that she wasn't able to play her "movie as a pro" for people. But how could she? The public comes into open houses for three reasons:

1. To see the home
2. To get information
3. To avoid the salesperson (!)

What does the public think about real estate salespeople? Generally, that one is as good as another. In training courses, I ask agents how they are different from the public's general view of a real estate agent. The reply is usually, "I'm an honest, enthusiastic, service-oriented professional." Then I ask the students how they *demonstrate* these qualities. The reply: "I demonstrate my qualities through the way I act with buyers and sellers." Here's the problem—people attending an open house want to avoid you, not get to know you. They will not give you the time to see you in the actions that prove your qualities. Unless you can *quickly* show them you are a cut above the generic agent, they will attempt an escape, just as they have with the other ten agents whose homes they have visited.

Project the Professional "You"

How do professionals in other fields demonstrate their professional selves? Envision your doctor's office. On the walls are diplomas that give you confidence about the doctor's qualifications. How do restaurants demonstrate—*before you eat the food*—that their food and service are good? Reviews from the newspaper and testimonials from customers are often displayed. You can inspire confidence in your services by adopting some of the same promotional strategies that successful professionals and businesses use. In this week's assignments, you were to start developing your professional portfolio. This serves two purposes:

1. It increases your confidence.
2. It shows buyers and sellers why they should choose you.

Screen Your Movie—Increase Your Confidence

Developing a portfolio provides an additional benefit. During the development process, you complete exercises that help you develop your unique approach to the business. You draw on your particular strengths, services, and business approaches that differentiate you from the generic agent. You then project these in a pictorial way to communicate added value to the potential client or customer. The result is an overall promotional strategy that will compete successfully in the marketplace. The best news for you, the new agent, is that this process helps develop your "movie" and greatly increases your confidence level.

■ Final Thoughts for Week Three

Remember, it's not the finished portfolio, but the process of thinking through your strengths, challenges, and competitors that is most important. In the highly competitive world of real estate sales and management, you must have a clearly, precisely defined picture of you as a "cut above." To compete, you must create, define, refine, and promote yourself masterfully. The bonus to you is that you will have created your "movie!"

Big Idea: Create a scrapbook of the future you.

■ Summary

You're further along your journey to a sale. You're gaining the habits that ensure success. Don't let your regular activities get boring. They *should* be getting predictable. You are learning the lead-generating habits of successful real estate agents. You're also gaining time-management and lead-generating habits that will propel you to a much higher career over the long term. (You won't really know that until you see yourself outselling those who started in the business the same time you did.)

On the business supporting side, you're adding sales skills and technical competencies, too. Keep practicing to get so competent you have mastery. In addition, keep working on all your systems and packaging. You should be working on them throughout your whole sales career.

Be sure to keep tracking and analyzing your contact ratios. Make adjustments quickly. Remember, your goal is a sale in your first four weeks.

Big Idea: Regularly doing lead-generating activities creates success habits for the long term.

Week Four Start-Up Plan

You are now approaching your final week in the *Up and Running* start-up plan. This week you will continue making the sales contacts to create early success. Because it's your last week in this plan, you get to choose the type of lead generating you will complete. You will refine your seller and buyer presentations. You will add to your professional portfolio. These systems should be on their way to being professional, polished, and practiced by now to ensure your success at every point of contact. (Note: As a pro, you will always be refining and tinkering with your systems. The objective in the first month is to get them to the point where you can use them as presentation guides.)

■ Week Four *Up and Running* Plan

These activities are all listed in your week four accomplishments in Section 12, Week Four forms.

Business Producing

30 Days to Dollars: Make 100 sales contacts using your favorite method or methods.

Get these results:
- Hold one public open house
- Secure two qualified buyer appointments
- Show homes to two qualified buyer groups
- Secure one appointment to do a listing presentation

- List one marketable property
- Sell one house

Time to stop and assess your ratios of lead generation to results. If you are not getting enough appointments, increase your lead generating.

These assigned activities are already in your spreadsheets, your *30 Days to Dollars* lead-generating plan, and your *30 Days to Dollars* lead-generating results for week four (in Section 12). All you need to do is to log in your actuals.

Business Supporting

Do these regular actions:

- Create your weekly schedule in advance of the following week (a blank form is in Section 12 for you)
- Add at least 50 contacts to your database
- Write at least 15 follow-up notes
- Evaluate your buyers and sellers using the buyers and sellers evaluation sheets (in Section 12)
- Do the activities in your marketing (follow-up) plan for this week
- Practice the sales skills assigned in this week
- Apply the sales skills that are assigned for this week in real life
- Follow your Technology Planner
- Add to your resource notebook
- Add to your attitude notebook
- Add to your office notebook

At the end of the week, measure your results using the four measurements below. Before your appointment with your manager,

1. use the daily planner,
2. evaluate your time management on your weekly schedule,
3. check off your completed activities on your weekly accomplishments, and
4. complete the goals/actuals spreadsheets weekly.

Additional business-supporting assignments include the following:

- Practice and apply sales skills #6 and #7 (from Section 10)
- Complete the entire listing process materials, including a market analysis package; include eight visuals to counter common listing objections
- Review and complete your qualifying/interview package for buyers, including visuals for countering buyers' eight most common objections

- Complete your personal promotional materials—a professional portfolio and/or your personal brochure
- Gain performance excellence in two new sales skills (you choose from the seven critical sales skills)
- Add three more visuals to counter objections sellers give you (to your seller presentation)
- Add three more visuals to counter objections buyers give you (put in your buyer presentation)

■ Summary

In your last week of *Up and Running*, you've had more freedom to create your own plan. You've chosen the kind of lead-generating activities that seem to work best for you. Because you've been doing so many lead-generating activities, you're able to analyze which are your best sources of business. You've also analyzed your ratios of leads to appointments to sales. Now you're starting to self-manage. You've also refined your various packages and presentations. This is the week you really have an opportunity to put it all together. If you've completed all the business-producing and business-supporting assignments during the program, you are far ahead of almost all the new agents who've started careers in the last year!

■ What You've Accomplished in Your Four Weeks

Congratulations! You have completed your first four weeks in the business. Not only have you finished (you might say "conquered") this program, you have formed the habits of successful self-management.

In business-producing activities, you have

- completed consistent, high-number contacts for prospects,
- qualified prospects for time management and control of your career, and
- sold one home and listed one home.

You have organized the support systems to the business to allow you to move faster:

- Listing process systems (including your market analysis)
- Technical knowledge: purchase and sale agreements, finance, market analysis
- System for qualifying/interviewing buyers
- Contact management system populated with all your contacts
- A budget and a time line for your professional management

- Resource notebook, office notebook, and attitude notebook for knowledge management
- Marketing plan
- Technology plan
- Personal promotional tools and plan
- Orientation procedures
- Tools of the trade

You have practiced sales skills in the office and "for real" in the field:

- Seven critical sales skills
- Four major types of lead-generating scripts

You have gained exceptional measurement and time management using

- a weekly planner,
- a daily planner,
- weekly accomplishments, and
- a goals/actuals spreadsheet.

Take *Up and Running* with You as You Excel in Your Career

Although we have portrayed this as your four-week plan, the business-producing part of the plan is actually a solid business-producing plan *for your entire career.* Now that you've had the opportunity to find your best sources of business, keep working them and measuring your results. Keep refining your systems and sales skills to build long-term mastery for a high-producing real estate career.

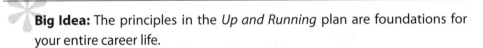

Big Idea: The principles in the *Up and Running* plan are foundations for your entire career life.

The Skills of Lead Generation

You've seen your four-week *Up and Running* plan. You're anxious about starting because you don't know how to make those sales calls. Sections 8, 9, and 10 are the training components of *Up and Running*. Here, I'll give you the skills you need to get into action (and only the critical skills—remember, this is not a training program!). In this section, I'll teach you the four approaches and scripts you need to make contacts with your best sources of leads. In Section 9, I'll show you how to "keep it going" to turn contacts into sales: how to qualify those leads so you know if they are good buyers or sellers and how to create and implement a marketing plan to follow up with them until they "buy or die." In Section 10, I'll teach you the seven most important sales skills I know you'll need to get more leads and convert them to buyers and sellers. Is that all the training you'll ever need? Of course not. You'll keep refining your skills and gathering more information for your whole career—I hope.

Big Idea: The most successful people in life are *always* challenging themselves to get better at what they do.

Why these particular skills? The sales skills and systems I'm sharing with you here are the *most important skills and systems* you need *right now* to get those sales and listings you want in your first year in the business. As you learn these skills, you may say to yourself, "These seem so easy and basic. Every agent must know and use them." Not true. These skills do seem easy to grasp, but, in the heat of the moment, without lots of practice and coaching, these skills get lost, and we just revert back to what is natural. Unfortunately, what's natural may not be effective *sales communication.*

Your best source of leads and how to contact them. To get your business off to a quick start, you will want to go to the best sources for leads. In this section, we'll discuss why I've chosen certain sources as best for you, along with the pros and cons of certain sources. I'll give you the training you'll need to jump right in. I'll show you how to make contacts to the four types of leads. I'll give you the scripts and letters you'll need to use. There's a lot of training in Section 8.

■ First: How Our Lead Generating Is Constructed

To create an effective lead-generating plan, follow these five principles of real estate marketing:

1. Segment your markets
2. Be proactive
3. Work the best sources
4. Work the numbers
5. Be frequent and consistent in your marketing

These are the principles we followed in creating your *30 Days to Dollars* lead-generating plan, a portion of the *Up and Running* plan.

Segment markets. The population explosion, information overload—these and other cultural developments make it impossible to promote yourself effectively to everyone. To be an effective lead generator today, you must *segment* and *prioritize* your potential markets. By segmenting your potential markets, you will discover certain best *targets.* A *target market* is a group of people defined through common demographics (i.e., age, income, real estate needs) and psychographics (i.e., lifestyle). To be an effective marketer, you need to clearly define your target markets and devise specific methods to sell to each. *30 Days to Dollars* segments markets and prioritizes them by *best sources of business.*

Be proactive. To be successful in real estate today, you must get most of your business from *proactive prospecting*—you go out and meet people. *30 Days to Dollars* uses mainly proactive activities. There are two kinds of lead generation:

1. Proactive—you go out and find people
2. Reactive—you sit and wait for people

You can control the number of leads you can get (and the money you make) only through *proactive* methods.

Work the best sources. To be successful, you'll want to start with your best sources of business. *30 Days to Dollars* prioritizes these sources for you.

Proactive sources include:

- Best—people you know
- Good—circle prospecting
- More challenging—for-sale-by-owner (FSBOs) and expired listings

These are the four lead-generating sources I'll teach you to contact in this section, in that order.

Why have I named *people you know* and *circle prospecting* the best sources for new agents? Because they

1. are least expensive (you don't have the money to spend on high cost lead generation);
2. are easy to work with and require few developed sales skills (you want results from your lead generating quickly—even before you develop sales skills);
3. are low rejection (new agents think they can take rejection, but are surprised and frustrated when they get dozens of "no"s);
4. have the biggest payoff for low cost and energy;
5. have little competition from other agents (people who already love you are more likely to work with you; when you go to a neighborhood to circle prospect, you're assured that very few other agents are willing to make the effort to meet potential customers face to face); and
6. build on the principles of correct lead generating priorities, so you'll keep these principles for your long-term business forever (experienced agents' best source of business is, again, people who think they're wonderful—those past customers and referrals).

Why are FSBOs and expired listings more challenging? They require great sales skills, tenacity, and ability to handle rejection. Most new agents are not quite skilled enough, and get so much rejection anyway that giving them more rejection their first month seems like cruel and unusual punishment!

Reactive sources include:

- Open houses
- Internet leads
- Relo leads
- Floor time

As a new agent, you may be relying on various reactive methods to get leads. Be sure to track your contacts vs. actuals in each of your sources using the goals/actuals spreadsheet so you'll know which are your best sources—and which are a waste of time for you.

Big Idea: To increase your success rate with reactive leads, master your qualifying and closing sales skills.

■ The Eight-Point Strategy to Turn Internet Leads into Sales

In the past few years, agents have become excited about Internet leads, a reactive source of business, only to be discouraged by them after they've gotten a few. Why? Because of the low conversion rates. According to Most Home Technologies, a lead management company, only one of 200 leads is converted to a sale. In addition, over 50 percent of the inquirers enter false data! Does that mean you shouldn't care about Internet leads? No. It means you must develop an Internet strategy to deal with these leads. Here's my eight-point strategy:

1. Have a rapid response method to any inquiry—according to a John L. Scott Real Estate survey, most inquirers want a response to an inquiry within two hours. Agents, on the other hand, took an average of 54 hours to respond, and only one half of the agents ever bothered to respond at all! If you're not interested in responding rapidly, don't count on capturing Internet leads.

2. Have a method to capture that lead's information immediately. You must use your database and contact management system diligently.

3. Have a method on your Web site that gives the potential client the information they want and lets them refine it.

4. Have the ability on your Web site to "lock them out" from more information unless they share their contact information with you.

5. Develop the skill of using "warm" language in your e-mail replies to portray yourself as an empathic human being. You need to humanize an otherwise cold medium.
   See the sample Internet reply note in Section 13.

6. Develop a method to go from "computer question and answer" to verbal communication. Think in terms of picking up the phone earlier rather than later. The only way you will form a relationship is to use one or more of the communication senses—hearing, seeing, or feeling. These aren't communicated via the computer!

The Eight-Point Internet Strategy

- Rapid response
- Capture the lead
- Screen the lead
- Interact with the lead
- Humanize your communications
- Go from keyboard (cold) to voice communication (warm)
- Develop sales skills
- Stay in touch forever

7. Develop the sales skills to turn that inquiry into a loyal client. (Don't just keep feeding them information. Ask good questions to find out their needs, then attach benefits. Ask them if those are the benefits they want. Finally, decide on their dominant buying motives and remind them of what they really want. See sales skills #2 and #7 in Section 9 for much more information on these skills and how to apply them in any situation.)

8. Be ready to stay in touch with this would-be client for many months to years. Most Home Technologies says that only 4–8 percent of Internet buyers obtained an online close within 90 days. (Mark Powell, founder of HouseValues, says that their research shows that over 28 months, 40 percent of those who made the first inquiry made a buying decision. This buying cycle is about three times longer than geographical farming. Be sure you're in it for the long run, not just for a quick sale.)

Resources to help you capture and manage your Internet leads. There are many companies offering services to provide Internet lead management. They include Bank of America Homeowners Services, Most Home Technologies, and Favoriteagent.com. In addition, some real estate franchises offer these management services. New agents should talk to their managers about which services they prefer. See the References section.

Big Idea: Spend most of your time and resources on your best sources.

Work the numbers. To be an effective marketer, you must make enough contacts to generate quality leads. *30 Days to Dollars* shows you which markets to target and how many calls you need to make—overall, 100 sales calls per week to ensure success—for one sale and one listing in your first 30 days in the business.

Big Idea: Lead generate as though your income depended on it—because it does.

But I'm Different

My main goal here is your success—your success in your first 30 days, not your first 30 years! So, if you don't have enough leads in the source I've assigned you in your *30 Days to Dollars* that week, go to another source. If you just despise contacting the source I assigned, substitute a source. If you find something doesn't work for you in your area, change the source. What you can't change: high numbers of contacts consistently. It surprises me how some agents and managers refuse to start the *Up and Running* plan because they believe in different source priorities. Bottom line: if you're convinced your source priorities work best for you in your area, I'm happy for you! Just get it done.

 Big Idea: Don't hide behind "I'm different" to avoid lead generating.

◾ How to Make Contacts in Each of the Four Lead-Generating Sources

This section shows you exactly how to make the sales call in each of the target markets in *30 Days to Dollars*. To make it easy for you to access, I've provided the scripts and letters for you to use, all saved in Section 13.

There are literally thousands of ways to make sales contacts and to follow up. I've chosen four approaches here that are easy to implement and get you results. But the best way is the one that works for you. Start with one method, and then make adjustments for your style and market area.

 Big Idea: The best method to make a contact is the method you prefer.

Practice makes perfect. Before you make a sales contact, craft your sales approach, using the sales skills described in this section and Section 10. Before you actually apply the sales skill in person, practice with your manager, a fellow agent, or your spouse, friend, or child—they will provide valuable feedback to help you be more effective in your actual sales calls.

◾ 1. Best Source of Business: People You Know

Many new agents look forward to letting people know they are in the real estate business. But, they don't know how to do it. I'd recommend you do a one-two punch:

A letter followed by a phone call.

Figure 8.1 is a sample of the letter you can use to write to your best lead-generating sources. It's also saved in Section 13 for you.

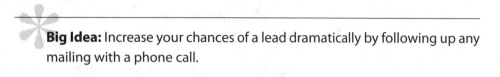

Big Idea: Increase your chances of a lead dramatically by following up any mailing with a phone call.

To *craft a sales call* (sales skill #1, to be applied in week one), use the following technique:

- Think of a particular person to call
- Determine a potential real estate need and benefit (sales skill #2, to be applied in week one) to this person

---

FIGURE 8.1   Letter: Introduction to People You Know

Dear _____,

I'm writing you this note to let you know I've just begun a new career. I'm now selling real estate with _____ [insert your company name]. It's an exciting profession, and I've already found that my background in _____ [fill in your pertinent background] has helped prepare me well for my new profession. In addition, I've had the benefit of attending a wonderful training program at our company, and I'm being coached by _____ [put in your manager or coach's name] so I'm getting the guidance and advice agents need to really be of service to buyers and sellers.

With all this knowledge and training behind me, I'm excited to help buyers and sellers. If you know of someone who wants to buy or sell in our area, please let me know. I'll give them the very best service I can, backed by the great reputation of my company and the support of my manager.

If I can answer questions about the state of the market for you, I'd love to do that, too. I'm keeping abreast of the market trends and prices in your area.

My contact information:

Your name
Office name
Office address

Phone
Fax
E-mail

Sincerely,

[your name]

Optimize your impact. Write a thank-you note after every visit.

- Write three questions to ask the person to discover these needs
- Determine your *call objective*
- Write a *question to get a lead* (sales skill #3, to be applied in week one) or appointment
- Write an opening statement

This method of crafting calls works for crafting any initial sales call. For example: Joe Smith is a family friend. A potential real estate need and benefit to Joe is a rental home, which will reduce his tax burden.

See Figure 8.2 for a worksheet to craft a call.

Three questions to ask Joe:

1. Is the equity in your present home enough to get a second mortgage to refinance for money to buy another home?
2. Have you thought about reducing your tax burden?
3. Have you looked into purchasing a home as a rental?

- The *call objective* is to get an appointment.
- The question to get the appointment is: when can we explore this potential?
- The opening statement is: I have been thinking about you. I'm in real estate now, and I have been exploring how to help people ease financial burdens with real estate.

Big Idea: This process, crafting a sales call, works for *any* type of lead!

FIGURE 8.2   Craft Your Own Sales Call to People You Know

Name of person: _____

Potential real estate need(s): _____

Benefit to the person of your service: _____

Three questions:

1. _____

2. _____

3. _____

Your call objective: _____

Question to get the order: _____

Opening statement: _____

Practice this sales call with a friend until you are comfortable.

FIGURE 8.3   A Script for Calling on People You Know

"Hi, Sally. I have been thinking about you. I'm in real estate now. Oh, you got my announcement postcard? Good. I've already learned to stay in contact frequently, since I guess agents aren't the best with that! Yes, I'm with ABC Realty, a wonderful firm in downtown Bellevue. Oh, you know that firm? Yes, I think I made a great decision. I wanted to call and let you know I'm working hard to do things right. I just got through my training school, and, boy, is there a lot to learn! It was great, though, and I feel really prepared to help people now. Yes, I have two sales and three listings so far. Yes, that's really great for a new agent! Also, I work with George Snell, who is my manager and coach. So, for these first few months, I have a real expert looking over my shoulder every step, which, I think, helps my clients feel comfortable. It's kind of a "two for one" benefit. Do you know anyone who needs my help? Great. [Take down the information. Ask who, when, where, can you use Sally's name.] Well, thanks again and I'll talk with you soon."

This script is also in Section 13 for your quick reference.
After the call, immediately

- send that handwritten note of thanks for the lead (see more below), then
- put that information in your database.

Big Idea: Be generous when thanking people for leads. Send a bouquet of flowers or a small book with your notated thanks. Remember, behavior that's rewarded is repeated.

Common mistake: Only rewarding people for a lead that results in a closed sale. You want to reinforce leads and motivate people to give you more of them!

What "no" means. Did you know that, on average, people say "no" to a salesperson four times before they say "yes"? But 96 percent of salespeople give up after the third no! (They quit right before that customer is ready to say "yes.") That's why tenacious agents always do so much better! I don't mean they are pushy (unless they have no sales communication skills at all!). I mean they understand it's human nature to say "no." They also know when it's in the customer's best interest to continue forward on the sales process. (Have you ever said "no" to something you wish you had said "yes" to?) Your job as a salesperson is to find a gracious method to *keep going.* Armed with the statistics I shared above, you will expect the "no," and have the next sentence ready.

Big Idea: "No" doesn't mean "no" forever. It just means "no" for now, or "I'm not ready." Or, "I don't trust you yet!"

A script to get referrals regularly. With people you know, ask: "Since I'm starting my real estate career, could I count on you to refer me to those who want to buy or sell? I'll touch base with you regularly."

A script to keep in touch. *Find a reason to keep in touch.* With people you know, ask: "Can I put you on my mailing list? We have a wonderful real estate newsletter that keeps you updated on the market so that you will have the latest in specific real estate information."

The Personal Note: Optimize the Power of That Call

After every conversation, no matter the lead source, follow up with a personal note, thanking that person for his or her time and looking forward to working with him or her in the future. See Section 13 for a sample note.

Big Idea: A personal note humanizes you against that Internet cold communication. Use handwritten notes generously. (As an agent, I always wrote more notes than anyone else in my office—and I was the number one agent in the office.)

■ 2. How to Circle Prospect

You've seen how to contact your best source of business, people you know. Now, we'll investigate your second source: homeowners in areas where you work. *Circle prospecting* means contacting homeowners in an area where you work—in person—to provide them with information about a property in their area. The object of circle prospecting is to get a lead.

You can circle prospect for these reasons:

- A new listing
- A house sold
- A listing sold

- An open house
- A price reduction

Why do it? As soon as a sign goes up in someone's yard, the people all around that sign start thinking about selling. The For Sale sign triggered a subconscious desire in other homeowners. Seasoned agents will tell you this: a For Sale sign always begets another For Sale sign. Why not be the agent of choice for those potential sellers?

How to get circle prospecting opportunities. You have no listings or sales. How are you going to get opportunities to circle prospect? Don't worry. If you're in a real estate office of any size, you have literally 60 to 100 opportunities per month to circle prospect. How? Just go to the agent who was the listing or selling agent for the reasons above. Ask that agent if you can circle prospect the property. Why? Successful, seasoned agents are too busy to circle prospect—or they're too lazy!

Big Idea: Put your circle prospecting strategy in your listing presentation to impress sellers with the fact you will *personally* promote their property.

Why Circle Prospecting Works

Circle prospecting works for several reasons:

1. Homeowners are curious about what is happening in their area.
2. Because few agents will take advantage of this opportunity, you have no competition with other agents!
3. Homeowners want to see an agent face-to-face—and are impressed that you took the time and energy to contact them in person.

How to choose the best area. This area should be one that you like, one that is closest to where you live or where you work, and one that homeowners will identify with you and your office. It should be one where you have several opportunities over time to get to know the homeowners. Circle prospecting, when done at a mastery level, is like geographical farming (getting to know the homeowners in a particular area over time). Except you are expanding your opportunities to several areas, and you have immediate reasons to call, so you'll get a lead faster.

When should you go? Find out the percentage of "workers" in your area. In many areas, both homeowners in the home work and are gone most of the day. Choose the time to go when they are home. Generally, after 5:00 PM or Saturday morning are the best times. Catching them doing yard work outside is great!

There are two important keys to success in circle prospecting:

1. Contact homeowners in person only—it's much more effective. Don't waste your money just sending a postcard! You want a *lead!*
2. Visit the same homeowner three times within a short period for different reasons so the homeowner will get to know and trust you. (Three possible reasons: the home is newly listed, there is an open house, the home sells.)

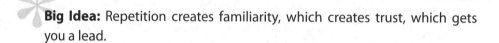

Big Idea: Repetition creates familiarity, which creates trust, which gets you a lead.

To prepare for circle prospecting, first decide on the reason why you are calling on the homeowner. Then create your materials, and design your script using the *craft a sales call* (sales skill #1) method.

The Outline of Your Call

1. Introduce yourself, and tell the homeowner why you are there. Be sure to include a benefit (sales skill #2) to the homeowner.
2. Ask the homeowner about the subject property: have you seen the Smith listing?
3. *Ask for a lead* (sales skill #3): Do you know anyone who . . . ? (indirect) Are you thinking of . . . ? (direct)

Advanced technique. Design your script to have a second question ready to follow up the first "no" (see indirect and direct questions example above). Let's say that your first question is: do you know anyone who . . . ? Your next question can be: are you thinking of . . . ?

The Circle Prospecting Script

See Figure 8.4. This script is also in Section 13 for your convenience.

Optimize your opportunity. Write a thank-you note within one day of your meeting, thanking them for their time and enclosing your card.

■ 3. How to Contact For-Sale-by-Owners

For-sale-by-owner listings (FSBOs) are an *immediate* source of business. After all, they let you know they are trying to sell their homes because they advertise and put up a sign! But they are also tough on salespeople. Why? They don't want to pay you a commission. They want to keep the

FIGURE 8.4   Circle Prospecting Script

"Hi. I'm Carla Cross with ABC Realty. We just listed the Smith home down the street. Have you seen the property? No? I'm going to be holding it open this weekend, and I'd love to invite you over. I'll even have coffee and cookies. I'm sure you'll be interested to see how the Smiths have creatively remodeled that trilevel. The listing price is $347,500. Here's a flyer with all the information and the open house date and time. By the way, [*ask an indirect or direct question to get a lead*]:

   Indirect: Do you know anyone in the area who has thought of selling?

   Direct: I see your home is one of the largest in the area. Have you thought about downsizing?

Thanks for your time. I'll check back, because I'll be letting you know when the property sells."

money. They may see you as competitors. They may not trust real estate agents. They may have had a bad experience. And they're kind of "sitting ducks" for salespeople. So, after dozens of aggressive real estate agents with few sales skills get through telling FSBOs things like "You're foolish to try to sell it yourself," you can bet they have learned to avoid all real estate people—and they're ready to avoid you, too.

About FSBOs. According to the National Association of REALTORS® survey, only 13 percent of all sellers sell their homes themselves (and about a quarter of those sales are to people they know). About half of the FSBOs said they wouldn't sell their own home again! So you have a "majority" opportunity, according to the statistics.

"Wimps" and "wimpettes" need not apply. Unfortunately, most agents who start making calls on FSBOs do it without developing the sales skills they need. They don't have a good method, and, after getting beaten up by a few FSBOs, just give up. This source is not for the wimpy! To contact and convert them to your listings, you must make this market a specialty and highly develop your sales skills over time. Because you're new, here's an approach that will work well you, because it's a low-rejection, low–sales skill approach. What it requires, though, is *consistency and organization*.

Big Idea: Calling on FSBOs successfully requires skill, tenacity, and consistency.

How to Find FSBOs

You don't have to do any research. Just watch for new FSBO signs in your area, or buy a service that tells you the new FSBOs each week. Or watch your local newspaper.

The recommended "drip" method. Surveys show that something happens with the FSBO property within six weeks: owners list their property, sell it themselves, or take it off the market. I've given you the process, along with what to say (the script) and the items to give, during this six-week time frame.

When doing this program, follow these rules:

- Make all sales calls in person. You want to form a relationship. You want to be their professional; you do not want to create an argument. You don't want to tell them they're stupid for trying to sell the home themselves!
- Go when the sign first goes up—the FSBO is still nice and eager to see anyone!
- Follow up consistently. You want to prove you are reliable; that you'll do what you say you will do. You will be one of the few agents who keep coming back!
- Give one new piece of information (not too much) each week. You want to show them you know your stuff. But you don't want to "give away the farm." Remember, the particular items aren't important. It's consistency that is important.

Here are some suggested items to bring when you call on an FSBO:

- Brochures from your title company (only one at a time)
- A list of tips to get your home ready for sale (can probably get from your title company or an inspection company)
- A list of what an inspector looks for (get from an inspection company)
- From a loan officer: items the purchaser will need to apply for a loan
- Two to three loan rate sheets from a mortgage company, to give the seller an idea of possible loans for buyers
- "How to Choose a Real Estate Agent" (complete with the help of your manager, or see the References section)
- "What I've Learned Selling Homes" (a document created by the agent)
- "What Buyers Are Looking for Today" (an article from your local newspaper)

- Articles about the market in your area (get from your newspaper)
- Time line: from sales agreement to closing (create with the help of your manager, or see the References section)

Figure 8.5 gives you a flowchart of this process.

Manager's Tip: Make an area of your office to keep these items. Ask your favorite mortgage provider, title company, escrow company, attorneys, inspectors, and so on to keep the area stocked. Now, your new agents don't have to stay in indecision to start this method!

As you give the item, ask if there is anything about the information you left the prior week that the seller needs help with. This is the excuse the sellers will give you when they are frustrated because they can't sell their own home. Now, make the appointment with both parties there.

On the appointment, answer questions and do your visual listing presentation.

Success rate. Using this program, studies show new agents can convert about *one out of five* sellers.

FIGURE 8.5   Converting FSBOs to Listings

Call/Time Frame	What to Say	What to Give
When sign first goes up	Introduce yourself: mention you saw sign; give materials to help you; I'll be back	One piece of buying/ selling information (see list in this section)
Week 2	Same as above; ask question about materials given*	Same
Week 3	Same	Same
Week 4	Same	Same
Week 5	Same	Same
Week 6	Same	Same

Objective: Make appointment to do listing presentation.

*This question is key to this system, because you need to give the seller a reason to invite you to meet him.

FIGURE 8.6 FSBO Script

First visit: "Hi. I'm Carla Cross with ABC Realty. I noticed your sign just went up. Selling your home? Great. I'd like to give you some information to help you. Why? We need "Sold" signs in the neighborhood to show buyers it's a very desirable place to live. Here's *[name the piece of information you're handing them]*. I know it will be useful to you because it *[fill in the benefits, using sales skill #2, explained in Section 10]*. I'll check in next week to see how it's going. Thanks for your time."

Second week and subsequent weeks: "Hi, Carla Cross again with ABC Realty. How's it going? *[Seller will probably tell you it's going great.]* Good. Was the information helpful that I dropped off last week? *[Seller probably won't remember what it was, but will tell you it was helpful.]* Great. Here's another item that I've found really helpful to sellers. *[Give them the item.]* I'll check back with you later."

Around week five: "Hi, this is Carla (oh, you remember . . .). How's it going? Is there anything about the information I've given you that I can help you with? Questions? *[Seller will, at this point, be getting desperate. He will use your question as a rationalization to invite you further.]* Okay. I'd love to answer that, but now is not a good time. I could come over tonight or tomorrow night. Which would be better for you and your husband? *[You want both parties there.]*

At the presentation: First, answer their questions. Then, go into your presentation. "I appreciate your time. Here's the answer . . . Let me show you how I work, so you'll have the benefit of choosing the right person should you decide to list your property. *[Now, do your listing presentation.]*" (See the References section for presentation help.)

The FSBO Script

Optimize your impression. Send a thank-you note within one day of your call or visit.

See Figure 8.6. This script is also in Section 13.

Other FSBO methods. You may want to take a more aggressive approach that requires a mastery of several sales skills. If so, see your manager for other methods. Your manager may have created a resource book of various methods to make these lead-generating contacts. Or, see an agent in your office who calls on FSBOs successfully. Don't get hung up on criticizing a particular method. Get the method you refer, practice the sales skills, make the first contact, and be consistent. Those are the principles that are most important.

■ 4. Listings That Have Expired

Do you know how to get a high customer satisfaction rating from a seller? (A high rating means you got done what the seller wanted done and she will refer you to many others.) No, it's not that you kept in touch. A huge survey from Consumer Reports showed sellers rated us high on customer satisfaction only when we

Get the home sold fast for close to full price

That doesn't say Get the home sold *slow,* or Get the home sold *way below listed price!* Expired listings are those listed by sellers who really wanted to sell at one time. But the agent took an overpriced listing. Now, that seller is a *dissatisfied* customer. And the seller whose home didn't sell within a short period of time isn't just mad at that particular agent and company—she's mad at all real estate companies! Your job, if you contact expired listings, is to turn around the perception of the seller and get that home listed at the right price.

Big Idea: At the right price, everything sells.

How to Contact Expired Listings

Your multiple listing service may give you expiration dates. If not, simply track the listings in the area you want to list. You'll want to target your efforts in areas where you can build your reputation as a person who gets homes sold.

Big Idea: Target FSBOs and expired listings in areas where you want to make a name for yourself. You need to build name recognition!

Contact right after the listing has expired. The best strategy is to contact the seller just after the listing has expired. If your MLS shows you expiration dates, preview the home prior to expiration so you have an idea of its condition. It is a violation of MLS rules to contact a homeowner to talk about listing his property during the term of the listing! But you can preview, and you should.

A different strategy: you may also try contacting those homeowners who gave up trying to sell their homes weeks or months before. They may be willing to give it another try now.

The *Up and Running* expired listing strategy. This is an approach that works well for the new agent, because it doesn't require aggressive sales

Optimize your impression. Send a thank-you note within one day of your call or visit.

skills and forms a good relationship with the seller. You are going to take the *survey* approach. You are going to contact the seller (either in person or by phone), and ask survey questions about the property. Your script is Figure 8.7, which is also in Section 13. By asking these questions, you will discover the problem areas of the prior listing, the seller's motivation, and the seller's degree of cooperation with you.

■ After the Conversation: Send a Pre-List Package with Your Thank-You Note

Immediately after hanging up, write a personal thank-you note and attach it to your pre-list package, which you will send that same day. Why? You want to prove to the seller that you are different: You follow up, you keep your word, and you actually communicate (the prior listing agent didn't, especially when the seller started calling because his listing wasn't selling . . .). This package can include the services you provide, your successful

---

FIGURE 8.7   *The Expired Listing Script*

Opening: "Hello. I'm Carla Cross of ABC Realty. Is your home still on the market? [*They may have re-listed and it isn't in your MLS yet.*] [*If no . . .*] Are you still interested in selling at some point? [*If yes, or maybe, or sometimes, even no*] I'll tell you why I ask. I work in this area, and would like to stay abreast of the properties available. In case I get a buyer for your home, I'd like to be prepared so your property is represented properly. Do you have about three minutes? [*If yes, go ahead. If no, ask, "What time would be convenient for me to give you a call?"*]

Questions: What do you feel are the biggest selling points of your home? That sounds like it should be attractive to many buyers! What kind of buyer do you feel would be attracted to your home? Why? Why do you feel it didn't sell? What do you feel was the best marketing the agent did? What would you have liked to see? If you were to list again, what would you be looking for in a listing agent? When and where are you moving? [*Use the "feel" words. Don't criticize the other agent. Just get the information and hum in agreement.*] [*If you don't have an opportunity to ask these questions, or you feel it isn't appropriate to ask all the questions on the phone, save them to ask at the appointment. You need to qualify this seller!*]

Close: It sounds as though you have a very sellable property if just a few adjustments are made. I'd love the opportunity to share my thoughts with you. [*If you have a successful track record, tell the seller now.*] I'm proud to say that I've helped [*or, our office has helped*] many sellers get their homes sold after they'd been unsuccessful with a different agent. Could I come over at [*time*] or [*alternate time*] when both of you would be home? It would take no more than 45 minutes, and you could tell me "not interested" at any time! If you decide not to sell your home at this time, at least you will have a different perspective. And hopefully you'll think of me if you decide to sell in the future."

track record (or that of your office), how you work, your professional portfolio (see Section 9), advice on selling their property, changing market trends, helpful hints to selling, and information on why now is the right time to buy. You can use many of the materials you have gathered to call on FSBOs. (For more information on creating a pre–first visit seller's package, see the References section and see your manager.)

At the home, ask any questions you didn't have an opportunity to ask. Then, do your listing presentation. Close for the listing.

Big Idea: Listing only homes that sell sets your professional standards high and ensures you create the success record FSBOs and expired listing sellers are seeking.

■ Summary

We've just provided the training you need, along with specific scripts, to make the four major types of lead-generating contacts. First, we began with the "why" behind the prioritized best sources of leads in this program. I want you to take these principles into your self-management throughout your whole career.

It's extremely important to your success that you start with these prioritized sources and keep your own numbers so you know your best sources for your long-term success. Too many times, new agents do a little of this, a little of that, and never master any one type of lead generation. So, they never learn what works for them.

In addition, I've provided the specific skills and scripts required in making these four types of lead-generating contacts. But you've only read them (and perhaps heard me role-play them on the CDs). To master these skills, you need to practice. You also need to apply them in the field dozens of times. You'll find you naturally gravitate to certain types of contacts and certain types of scripts. Make them your own, and no market will ever conquer you. You'll conquer it!

Big Idea: Practicing and applying these sales skills dozens of times in the field makes the difference between low and high payoffs for your efforts.

In the next section, we'll look longer term at your business and discuss some of the business-supporting systems you'll want to put into place now:

1. An evaluation system for your leads—so you choose to work with the right people (a great time management tool)
2. A marketing plan—your system to keep in touch until they "buy or die"
3. Your professional portfolio, the most important piece of self-promotion you'll need right now (to gain the confidence of buyers and sellers)

Must-Haves in Your Sales Arsenal: Qualifying Procedures, Marketing Plans, and Your Personal Promotional Tool

You've seen the four-week plan. You're starting the plan. You have the scripts for lead generating. Now, you need three other systems to turn those leads into sales:

1. A qualifying system for your leads—so you choose to work with the right people (a great time-management tool)
2. A marketing plan—your system to keep in touch until they "buy or die"
3. A self-promotion tool—your professional portfolio (to gain the confidence of buyers and sellers)

■ Qualifying Buyers and Sellers for Effective Time Management

According to new agents, the most difficult challenge to master is *time management.* For many, problems with time management stem from agents' not qualifying buyers and sellers. Not everyone should be put in your car and shown homes! Before you ever put a buyer in your car or go to a listing presentation, ask yourself, "Is doing this in my best interest?" Usually the new agent's motto is, "I'll work with anyone." Unfortunately, adopting that attitude leads to bad habits, wasted effort, and disappointment over those buyers and sellers who refuse to close. To help you get you off on the right foot, create the kind of judgments great agents make, and spend your time effectively, I have created four tools. Following them will force you to look before you leap. These qualifiers teach you where to draw the line. I call these your *professional standards; that is,* what you will and won't put up with!

Professional standards. Here are some examples of situations in which you need to have these standards in place:

- Would you put a buyer in your car who wouldn't meet with you for an hour first?
- Would you work with a buyer who wouldn't be loyal?
- Would you work with a buyer who wouldn't be honest with you?
- Would you list an overpriced home?
- Would you do a buyer or seller presentation without all parties present?

You will see many more areas in my evaluators that help you think through these situations and decide where to draw the line so you don't waste your time and money—or get taken advantage of. By the way, everyone has professional standards, even if they didn't have the benefits of thinking through them like you do here. Their standards are simply what they allow!

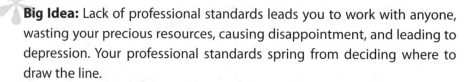

Big Idea: Lack of professional standards leads you to work with anyone, wasting your precious resources, causing disappointment, and leading to depression. Your professional standards spring from deciding where to draw the line.

Your tools for buyers:
1. Tracking qualified buyers
2. Qualified buyer evaluator

Your tools for sellers:
1. Listing presentation qualifier
2. Marketable listing evaluator

The Two-Step Process

Many times we're so happy to snag a buyer or seller that we forget to take it one step at a time. Here's the model I want you to use to qualify buyers and sellers. Think of the job interview process. The interviewer asks lots of questions to the interviewee. If the interviewee's answers warrant, the interviewer then sells the interviewee. It's no different in the process of working with buyers and sellers (you are the interviewer):

- Interview first (use the questionnaires in this section)
- Sell second

Figure 9.1 is a graphic representation of how to arrange your presentation.

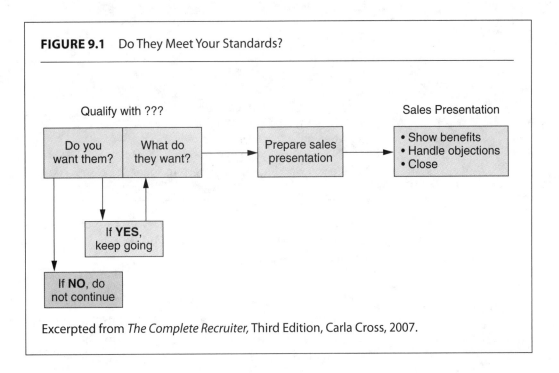

FIGURE 9.1   Do They Meet Your Standards?

Excerpted from *The Complete Recruiter,* Third Edition, Carla Cross, 2007.

In this section, we're going to explore the first part of the process: the interview.

Buyers First

Ask questions and make judgments with your professional standards. New agents work with more buyers than sellers as a rule, so we'll tackle qualifying buyers first. How do you avoid working with those you really don't want to work with? Qualify them. What does that mean? Ask questions first before you put buyers in the car. Listen to how these buyers answer and compare those answers to your professional standards. I'll share with you some qualifying questions you should ask and show you how to use the evaluators for buyers.

Using the "quick questionnaire." You will meet buyers "on the fly," such as in open houses or from an incoming floor call. You need to have your quick qualifying questions ready. They can include:

- How long have you been looking for a home?
- What attracted you to this home?
- When do you want/need to move?
- Have you been prequalified by a lender?
- Are you working with a real estate agent?

Figure 9.2 is a short questionnaire you can use when you need it. Have it with you at all times so you won't forget to ask these questions—and save

---

FIGURE 9.2   Quick Qualifying Questionnaire for Buyers

- How long have you been looking for a home?
- What attracted you to this home?
- When do you want/need to move?
- Have you been prequalified by a lender?
- Are you working with a real estate agent?

---

yourself time and money so you don't pick people who aren't motivated or who already have an agent!

Qualify the buyer first for these things:

- Motivation
- Needs
- Ability to buy
- Ability to be loyal to you

The buyer consultative session. You aren't going to be able to do a credible job unless you take the time to sit down with the prospective buyer and do a consultative session using a comprehensive buyer questionnaire. The consultative session is a meeting, about an hour long, during which you educate the buyer on buying today and ask qualifying questions. Here are two essential components of the process:

1. *Your buyer's questionnaire.* To appear professional, have a questionnaire ready for every buyer so you can be get all the answers you need prior to showing homes. See the References section for a comprehensive program for working with buyers, and see your manager. She may have a comprehensive program and/or questionnaire already.
2. *Your buyer presentation.* You will use this presentation to stay on track during your consultative session. It will contain the same kinds of things as your seller presentation. See your manager for company materials and suggestions about what can go into your buyer presentation.

I told you *Up and Running* is not a training manual, and this is one topic that can't be taught adequately here. To become a competent buyer's agent, you need to take a real in-depth course on buyer representation and gather the professional materials to represent buyers professionally.

Tracking Qualified Buyers

Figure 9.3 is a tracking tool so you can be sure you are working with enough qualified buyers. It's also in Section 12 because you're going to use it weekly for effective time management.

As a new agent, your job is to gather as many qualified buyers as quickly as you can. This tracking tool helps you see how you're doing. Every time you qualify buyers, add them to your sheet. Check off that you used the

FIGURE 9.3   Tracking Qualified Buyers

Record and qualify your buyer leads

Date of Qualifying Meeting	Name	Address	Questionnare Used?	Both @ Qualifying Session?	# Showings	Sales

Excerpted from *The Complete Buyer's Agent Toolkit*, Carla Cross Seminars, Inc.

questionnaire and that they were both at the session. Keep track of the number of showings (the number of times you take them to look at homes, not the number of homes shown). Estimate when they will buy so you have a sense of your potential income. Finally, log in when you sold them. Share this information with your manager in your weekly coaching meeting.

Using the Buyer's Potential Evaluator

Figure 9.4, Buyer's Potential Evaluator, is a tool you'll be using every week for effective time management. It's in Section 12 for your weekly use.

I love this tool because it forces agents to evaluate the worth of that particular buyer to them. Take a look at the areas I've listed. These are the areas where you need to set boundaries. Take the evaluator and decide your own boundaries. Add other boundaries that are important to you. Now, add to my questionnaire the questions you would need to ask to find out whether buyers meet your professional criteria. Don't be afraid you won't get any business. It's human nature to want the very best. You are choosing them, as they are choosing you!

What happens without standards? Many agents think that they will "get tough later." Bob (not his real name), an agent in my office, refused to qualify buyers. He simply tried to talk to them between showing homes while driving them around. He told me he intended to start doing a better job of qualifying them when he was more successful. Bob lasted in the business only a few months. He felt people took advantage of him. He had trouble closing; he kept trying to find the "magic words" to make buyers do what he wanted. He thought memorizing closing techniques would solve his buyer problems. In truth, though, great qualifying makes those old-style manipulative closing techniques worthless (and, good riddance!). Bob's refusal to set professional standards and lack of results led to depression and lowered self-esteem until he *shrunk* out of the business.

Big Idea: Become a great qualifier, and your troubles with closing will disappear.

But, I'm afraid I won't have anyone to work with . . . Yes you will, if you increase your lead generating. Start right—prospect for hundreds of potentially qualified prospects. Then, be tough when you qualify them.

Big Idea: The cure for not closing prospects is more lead generating, not more closing skills.

FIGURE 9.4   Buyer's Potential Evaluator

Rate on a scale of 1–4 (4 is the highest)

1. Buyer answered all qualifying questions.	1	2	3	4
2. Buyer is motivated to purchase. (Rate each spouse/partner separately.)	1	2	3	4
3. Buyer is realistic about price range expectations.	1	2	3	4
4. Buyer is open and cooperative.	1	2	3	4
5. Buyer will purchase in a timely manner.	1	2	3	4
6. Buyer is a referral source and will provide referrals.	1	2	3	4
7. Buyer has agreed that you will be his or her exclusive agent.	1	2	3	4
8. Agent has established a positive rapport with buyer.	1	2	3	4
9. Buyer will meet with loan officer.	1	2	3	4
10. Buyer answered financial questions openly.	1	2	3	4
11. Buyer has no other agent obligations.	1	2	3	4
12. If buyer has home to sell, he or she is realistic about price.	1	2	3	4
13. Buyer will devote sufficient time to purchasing process.	1	2	3	4
14. Both spouses/partners will be available to look for home.	1	2	3	4
15. This buyer is worthy of my time, energy, and expertise.	1	2	3	4

Use this evaluator with each buyer to ensure you are working within your standards to achieve effective time management and referrals.

Excerpted from *The Complete Buyer's Agent Toolkit*, Carla Cross Seminars, Inc.

Qualifying Sellers

Following is a common scenario for new agents (even some experienced agents still fall into this trap): a prospective client calls during your floor time and requests a market analysis on his home. You're so excited that you make an appointment without asking any qualifying questions. You inspect the home and do all the work required to complete a market analysis. You return to the home and give the prospective client your complete, full-color, 20-page market analysis. You don't hear from him. You call and find out that he wanted the market analysis to give to his niece, who just entered the real estate field, for an assignment in her training school. You feel used. However, the prospective client feels, because you provided the market analysis service without qualifying him, he got what he wanted. And he assumes that you got what you wanted. *Was* it what you wanted? Don't think so.

Big Idea: As a professional, it's your job to teach the seller how you work.

The two-step qualifying process.   To list a property, use a two-step process, just like the process for qualifying buyers:

1. *Qualify* the seller and the property for salability.
2. *Present* your marketing plan, including pricing, to the seller.

Remember that flowchart, Figure 9.1, excerpted from *The Complete Recruiter?* All real estate professionals, from agents to managers, need to use the same process—in the same order—to qualify any of our "candidates." Apply this flowchart to qualifying sellers as you did with buyers.

Start Qualifying on the First Phone Call

Qualifying starts in the first phone conversation with the seller. The agent needs to find out the following:

- When do you want/need to move?
- Where are you moving?
- Have you ever sold a home before?
- What are you looking for in a listing agent?
- Can I come over and preview the home and visit with you?

I've collected these questions into a questionnaire for you (Figure 9.5) so you can have it ready on the fly. Be ready *not* to go on that appointment if they don't meet your standards!

Big Idea: Prepare your "knockout" factors—those answers sellers give you that cause you to not want to go further. Those knockout factors become your *professional standards*.

FIGURE 9.5   Quick Qualifying Questionnaire for Sellers

- When do you want/need to move?
- Where are you moving?
- Have you ever sold a home before?
- What are you looking for in a listing agent?
- When can I come over and preview the home and visit with you?

After the phone call and before the appointment. Stand out from the crowd! Send a thank-you note along with your pre-list package (see the References section, or ask your manager for ideas about what can go in the package). This is one of those comprehensive areas that can't be adequately covered in *Up and Running*. However, there are fine training programs on listing practice and excellent listing process packages.

Before you go to the appointment. Enter your potential clients in your Listing Presentation Qualifier (Figure 9.6) and start evaluating the sellers. Track each of the sellers with this checklist and share it with your manager during your weekly coaching meeting. Use it, too, to hold to your professional standards. This is in Section 12 because you'll be using it each week for time management.

The Consultative Meeting at the Sellers' Home

What should you do first as you meet the seller at his home? Qualify him! Why walk around the home if the seller isn't going to meet your professional standards? To prepare the seller for how you're going to work, explain the process. Here's your script:

"So I can get to know you, Mr. Seller, I have some questions to ask you. Then, I'll walk through the home with you so you can show me your home's features."

The comprehensive client questionnaire. You will need to develop a much more comprehensive client questionnaire. See your manager or the References section.

How a top agent works. Let's look at an agent who's made a tough, professional personal boundary of not listing properties she has determined will not sell in normal market time. This agent will not list properties that are more than 3 percent over her analysis of what that property will actually sell for. Why this personal boundary? This "pro" wants to

FIGURE 9.6   Listing Presentation Qualifier

Date of Presentation	Name	Address	Want to Sell?	Both Home?	2 Hours Pre-Scheduled?	How Much $ Want?	Marketing Presentation Completed?	Results

Excerpted from *Your Client-Based Marketing System*, Carla Cross Seminars, Inc.

establish a name for herself as a REALTOR® who only lists properties that sell. Her reputation depends on "sold" signs on properties. Obviously, this reputation will attract only serious sellers who appreciate her professional attitude. During the first appointment, if she determines that the sellers want more money for their home than her initial professional opinion indicates, she will not make the next appointment. Why should she waste her time and ruin her reputation? Or, if after the second appointment the sellers want more money for their home than her expert opinion warrants, she won't list the home.

Recently, I saw how this strategy works. An agent in my office prepared a marketing plan for a seller. However, because the competition priced the property $50,000 higher than our agent, the seller chose to list with the competition. Unfortunately, the competition did not work in our area and used the wrong homes to diagnose the home's selling challenges.

Initially, the seller was pleased with the listing agent because he listed the home at such a high price. Of course, the seller expected selling agents to bring customers. However, agents who wanted to create trust and loyalty with their buyers would not show the overpriced home to their buyers. So the seller saw few potential buyers.

After three months of lost marketing time, the disillusioned seller listed with our agent at the right price. However, irreparable damage had been done to all parties involved. National surveys show that this added time on the market costs the seller thousands of dollars. Homes that are on the market a long time sell for less than if they were listed at the right price and sold quickly. (Remember Charles Revson's marketing truism: Create demand. When buyers compete, the price goes up.) Because the first listing agent did not create a satisfied customer, he or she will not get any return business. Unfortunately, the agent who lists the home the second time around won't have as satisfied a customer as if he had been able to list the home first—at the right price.

Big Idea: Overpricing properties causes negative results for sellers and a negative perception of our industry.

Using the Marketable Listing Evaluator. Figure 9.7 is an evaluator to ensure you are qualifying sellers to your standards. It's also in Section 12 because you'll be using it each week for effective time management.

Sellers qualify agents. And good agents carefully qualify sellers. How confident would you feel if your doctor did not ask you any questions but simply prescribed aspirin every time you came to the office?

FIGURE 9.7   Marketable Listing Evaluator

---

1. Property listed at competitive price   Yes_____   No_____

2. Full-term listing agreement   Yes_____   No_____

3. Seller to complete obvious repairs/cleaning prior to showing   Yes_____   No_____

4. Easy access (e.g., key, phone for showing)   Yes_____   No_____

5. Yard sign   Yes_____   No_____

6. Immediate possession   Yes_____   No_____

7. Extras included (e.g., appliances)   Yes_____   No_____

8. Available for first tour   Yes_____   No_____

9. FHA/VA terms available   Yes_____   No_____

10. Owner financing available   Yes_____   No_____

11. Below market down payment   Yes_____   No_____

12. Below market interest rate   Yes_____   No_____

13. Post-dated price reduction   Yes_____   No_____

14. Market commission   Yes_____   No_____

15. In my evaluation, this property will sell within listed market range,
     in normal market time for this area.   Yes_____   No_____

16. I will receive referrals from the sellers.   Yes_____   No_____

Use this evaluator with each of your potential listings to ensure sellers meet your standards.

Excerpted from *Your Client-Based Marketing System*, Carla Cross Seminars, Inc.

Sellers' confidence in an agent is raised when they know that the agent has established certain criteria for marketing property. Why waste sellers' time—and money—if the property won't sell? Answering the questions on the Marketable Listing Evaluator with each potential listing ensures you establish your professional boundaries.

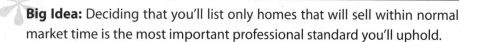

> **Big Idea:** Deciding that you'll list only homes that will sell within normal market time is the most important professional standard you'll uphold.

■ Building Your Marketing Plan

It's not over after your first contact! We discussed the fact that buyers take longer than ever from that first inquiry to their buying decision. That means you must stay in touch—until they "buy or die." That means you must create a marketing plan for those you have met. You must become "top of the mind" to them so, when they are ready to make a buying decision, they work with you.

Frequency and Consistency Are Key

Here are two truisms from the world of marketing you need to grasp to design a good marketing plan:

1. Frequency is more important than reach.
2. Consistency is everything.

> **Big Idea:** Frequency + Consistency = Success

The first truism means that it's much more effective to contact fewer people frequently than to contact many people just a few times. So don't spend money mailing one card once to a thousand strangers. Don't spend thousands of dollars once to put an ad in your Sunday newspaper saying you are the greatest. Instead, contact those who already know you or hear of you frequently and consistently.

Consistency is key. One of the mistakes agents make in their marketing plans is that they send a great big newsletter to their contact list once a year. That's not consistency. Consistency means communicating with them at least monthly. Some marketing experts suggest communicating with them weekly for the first few weeks. Then go to monthly. Why? It takes frequent, consistent communication for the potential client to recognize and remember you.

Designing Your Marketing Plan

Sit down now and write how you will communicate with those you already know frequently and consistently. That may include the following:

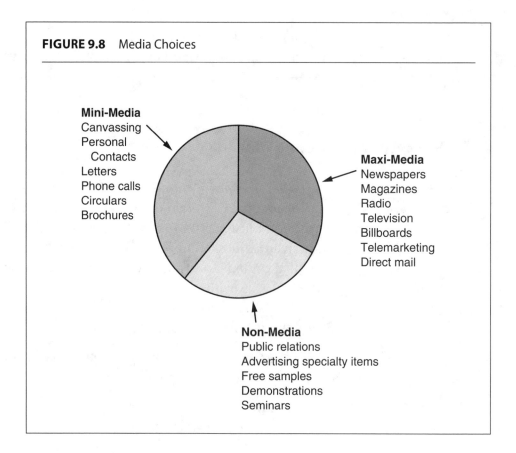

FIGURE 9.8   Media Choices

Mini-Media
Canvassing
Personal
   Contacts
Letters
Phone calls
Circulars
Brochures

Maxi-Media
Newspapers
Magazines
Radio
Television
Billboards
Telemarketing
Direct mail

Non-Media
Public relations
Advertising specialty items
Free samples
Demonstrations
Seminars

- Postcards
- Letters
- Newsletters
- E-mails
- Personal visits
- Gifts
- Telephone calls
- Parties

Your Media Choices

The figure above gives you an easy way to look at some choices. Which category do you think are lowest cost? Non-media and mini-media. Start there. Why? You have time but no money! Also, you are in a personal-service, relationship business. Use the marketing strategies that get you in front of people to reinforce the qualities you want them to recognize about you.

Proving you made the transition to real estate sales. How will you prove to people who knows you as a musician, for example, that you are now a capable real estate professional? Remind them over and over that you are successfully selling real estate. Mailings to these people are easy. They are the same mailings you are doing to promote properties. Each time you have a brochure or flyer on a property you or someone in your office has listed, merely drop that flyer in the mail with a note: "Just wanted you to know the latest in property values," "Just wanted to keep you abreast of the market," "Thought this property would fit some of our friends," or "Please pass on this information to someone you know." By sending the flyer you are teaching your friend that you are actively engaged in selling real estate. You are also showing your friend that, over time, you are accountable for keeping in touch in a professional way.

Your Complete Marketing Plan

You're not done with your marketing plan until you've decided the what, who, how, and how much—for a year. For example, at the end of the year, as part of my business plan for my speaking, coaching, and product businesses, I design a marketing plan that consists of mailings, newsletters, e-mails, personal calls, and gifts. Then, I attach a budget and assign names to carry out the plan. I schedule each of these events in my Goldmine (my contact management program). Now I don't have to scramble every month to decide how I'm going to keep in contact with my best sources of business. It's all planned for the whole year. My team and I work on the monthly marketing tactics so we stay in touch with you . . . forever!

After you've designed your plan, put your activities in your contact management system so they will drive you.

A Worksheet Marketing Planner for You

Figure 9.9 is an example plan I created so you can plan your ongoing marketing. I've provided you a blank marketing planner in Section 12 so you can create your own plan. After you create your plan, set a date on which to have each of your marketing materials/scripts ready to use. Finally, put each of these dates in your contact management system so you'll remember to do it!

Big Idea: Schedule implementation of your marketing plan.

Enlist the Experts to Help You Create Your Marketing Plan

As a new agent, I urge you to use some premade materials and plans, such as those available from The Personal Marketing Company, Prospects

FIGURE 9.9   Your Marketing Plan

1. Name your target market (who you're marketing to).
2. Put your actions in order of the dates to be accomplished.
3. Assign work to be accomplished in each tactic. Add your budget figure.
4. Tally your total budget from this target market.

Target Market: _____

Action	Assigned To	To Be Done By	Budget
Introduction	agent	1st month (Jan)	200 people @ 50 cents = $100
Phone calls (ask for referrals)	agent	2nd month (Feb)	200 people @ 25 cents = $50
e-Newsletter (one page)	agent	1st–2nd month (Feb)	200 people @ 25 cents = $50
"Spring Ahead" postcard	agent	3rd month (Mar)	200 people @ 30 cents = $60
Personal visit—seeds for spring plants	agent	4th month (April)	200 people @ 50 cents = $100
e-Newsletter (one page)	agent	5th month (May)	200 people @ 25 cents = $50
"Just Listed" postcard	agent	6th month (June)	200 people @ 30 cents = $60
Phone calls (ask for referrals)	agent	7th month (July)	200 people @ 25 cents = $50
e-Newsletter (one page)	agent	8th month (Aug)	200 people @ 25 cents = $50
"Just Sold" postcard	agent	9th month (Sept)	200 people @ 30 cents = $60
Personal visit—pumpkins	agent	10th month (Oct)	200 people @ $1 = $200
e-Newsletter (one page)	agent	11th month (Nov)	200 people @ 25 cents = $50
Holiday card	agent	12th month (Dec)	200 people @ 50 cents = $100

Notes:

E-Newsletter 4 times/year; preprinted postcards 3 times/year

Regularly send anniversary cards to each person you sold

Take housewarming gift within 2 weeks after closing (to both buyers and sellers)

Increase your postcards (just listed/just sold) as you can, to prove you are a successful agent

Excerpted from *The Business Planning System for the Real Estate Professional*, Carla Cross Seminars, Inc.

Plus, and in Top Producer. Your company may have marketing pieces and copy you can use, too.

Remember: your job is to get your face and name in front of those who already know something about you, over and over again. Your job is not to spend lots of money in low payoff items!

Big Idea: Heroes aren't those who make their own marketing plan. Heroes are those who implement the plan and get results.

■ Marketing *You*

You've found out how to set your professional standards. You have the information and forms to qualify buyers and sellers for effective time management. You know now how to build a marketing plan. You're almost done with your "people management" systems. The last thing you need to do is to develop your professional portfolio. You need a method to stand out from the crowd. You need a method to build your confidence and self-esteem so you can better build your business.

What the Portfolio Is For

Experienced agents have a track record of success. They can tell buyers and sellers about how they listed properties that sold, how they sold 50 homes the prior year, and so on. Because you're new, you don't have that track record. Can you compete? Yes. How? By showing the prospective buyer your lifelong successes, talents, skills, and values.

What is a professional portfolio? It's a pictorial of *you,* your background, your skills, your hobbies, and your talents, with letters of recommendation from those who know and trust you. It's like a movie of you! Only it's not expensive to produce like a movie.

Big Idea: The portfolio speaks volumes for you so you don't have to brag.

Why a Portfolio Works

As a new agent, I had no successes. I hadn't even been in a field closely related to real estate! So, what did I have? At first, I was actually bereft. I didn't feel I had anything to offer. But as I thought about it, I realized I had taken with me into real estate my lifelong achievements. What I knew about myself was that I had to have been dutiful, responsible, and accountable to have practiced piano regularly all through college and held a job requiring 12 hours of work a week while still finding time to study. I knew I could handle several things at once—a skill certainly required in real estate. Also, I knew I had become a pretty good negotiator from having to negotiate fees for music jobs. What I needed to do was to demonstrate those same skills to my friends in a new business. That's how I came up with the idea of the portfolio.

Big Idea: The portfolio builds trust and confidence in buyers and sellers.

What a Portfolio Looks Like

Picture a top-of-the-line three-ring binder. Inside, you'll have stationery dividers—title pages that introduce you. Inside each of those sections, you'll include pictures, letters, diplomas, testimonials—the list is almost endless of the evidence you can use to show people who don't know you and what you bring to real estate that benefits them. Cost: less than $20 per portfolio. Value: invaluable!

How to Create Your Portfolio Contents

Complete the portfolio exercise in Figure 9.10. Ask yourself, "What skills do I bring from my former career, business, avocation, etc.? What are the benefits of these skills to buyers and sellers? How can I show it?"

After you've brainstormed this information, start throwing all kinds of evidence in folders with your divider page names. (See the References section for a complete guide.)

How to Use the Portfolio

Make several portfolios, because you're going to need them. You'll be so busy! Use them in these situations:

1. Open houses—have one open on the counter
2. Pre–first visit buyer package—include it, and pick it up when you do your qualifying and presentation
3. Pre–first visit seller package—include it, and pick it up when you do your qualifying and presentation

FIGURE 9.10   Portfolio Exercise

List Your Skills	Benefits to Buyers/Sellers	Show It—Evidence

Other Benefits

Sometimes we need to be reminded of our value. That's the time to read your own portfolio. It raises our self-confidence and fights those negative feelings we get when we are rejected time after time. It forms the basis for other promotional pieces, like brochures. It gives you a wealth of information from which to draw your marketing strategies. It absolutely allows you to compete with the "big guys" successfully. (I know. All my top first-year agents created portfolios and used them to get listings and buyers against multi-million-dollar producers!)

■ Summary

You've learned the three tools you need to build the rest of your career strategy:

1. A qualifying system for your leads—so you choose to work with the right people (a great time-management tool)
2. A marketing plan—your system to keep in touch until they "buy or die"
3. A self-promotion tool—your professional portfolio (to gain the confidence of buyers and sellers)

You've gotten the forms and checklists that are really built-in self-management training tools (and you didn't even know I was training your mind!). You're building your systems so you can go fast and do well. Next: the seven critical sales skills you need to master to lead generate, qualify, handle objections, and sell.

Seven Critical Sales Skills for Success

Yes, you can sell homes to people without having effective sales skills. But it will take you much more time and much more money to do it than if you had mastered sales communication. In this section, I'll show you how to communicate with your potential buyers and sellers so you sell more homes more often. But, there's one ingredient I can't provide in this resource:

Practice

It's great you're reading about these sales skills. But reading about them doesn't mean you can do them. In each week of the four-week plan, you'll see I've assigned you practice for each of these sales skills areas. I've also suggested specific practices for you in each of the seven sales skills explained here. Why? Without practice, you'll just be able to say, "I heard that before." I've heard lots of piano concertos before, too, but that doesn't mean I can play them! So, read each of these, and take seriously my assignment of practicing each of these skills until you are an *unconscious competent*. That means when you are in a situation that requires using one or more of these skills, you unconsciously use the one you need at the time.

 Manager's Tip: In this section, I've provided you a sample practice session for each of the seven critical sales skills. Teach one per sales meeting and get your agents practicing each one that week. Now you have expanded *Up and Running* into training.

■ Why These Particular Skills?

Because they are the most critical to your early success. I picked them from dozens of sales skills because you need these particular skills *right now!* These are the skills taught in every sales skills development program throughout the world of business. I know, because I've spent thousands of dollars learning them! They are also the skills that few real estate salespeople develop. Why?

1. Most real estate salespeople get focused on learning everything they can about finance, law, inspection, and so on. The technical points. That's because they are afraid of not knowing everything. In addition, most training programs in real estate companies are heavy on these technical subjects and contain very little or no sales training. New agents think memorizing facts and laws assure their success. Yes, knowing how to fill in the blanks on purchase and sale agreements is important. But we're working with *people*. Making money in our business depends 95 percent on our sales communication skills with people. We must develop great sales communication skills if we want to be successful—and help buyers and sellers make good buying decisions.

2. If these sales skills are covered in training programs, it's usually just a mention. Or, the only person doing the skill is the trainer. Agents don't have an opportunity to practice in class until they are "killer" at them.

Big Idea: Master these seven critical sales skills to increase your income and lessen your time and effort.

The Scripts

In this edition, I've added a section just for the scripts you've seen. See Section 13, which also has several sales letters and sales forms. These are *training* bonuses for you!

Using These Skills for Reactive Leads

As I explain each of these skills, I'll be showing you how to apply them with reactive leads: open houses, floor time, and Internet leads, for example. These skills work in all sales situations!

> **Big Idea:** Learn each sales skill and relate it in context to all your selling situations, not just one (e.g., the "hum" technique works as you meet people in all lead-generating situations).

■ The Seven Critical Sales Skills

Here are the major sales skills you need to master right now to get a sale quickly. Each of these skills is introduced during your four weeks, and you have an assignment to practice them as they are introduced.

1. *Craft a sales call script.* This works to craft any type of sales call—the one to people you know, the one to the FSBO, or the one to the expired listing. This sales skill is to be applied with your first lead-generating source, people you know, in week one.

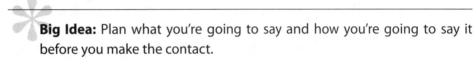

> **Big Idea:** Plan what you're going to say and how you're going to say it before you make the contact.

2. *Attach benefits.* Show customers that there is something in it for them. Too often, salespeople only think of what a sale will do for them, not what it will provide for the buyers of their services! This sales skill is practiced and applied in week one.

> **Big Idea:** Decide "what's in it for them" and verbalize that at every opportunity so you remind yourself it's not about you!

3. *Ask a question to get the order.* This skill is used in every situation where you want to get a lead. It seems simplistic, but too often salespeople fail to ask for the order. To ensure that you get a lead, craft and apply this simple yet critical sales skill in all sales situations. This sale skill is introduced in week one.

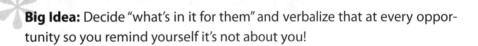

> **Big Idea:** If you don't ask, you don't get.

4. *Use the AAA method of objection-busting.* This method of crafting a process to counter, defuse, or anticipate objections is critical to each

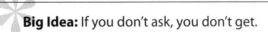

sales situation. In truth, all salespeople encounter objections and rejections with each sales call. With the AAA method, you learn to craft a whole process to take objections from an adversary relationship to a discussion. Use this method, introduced in week two, to qualify buyers and sellers, and throughout the entire sales cycle. For more skill building in answering objections, see the References section.

Big Idea: Answering an objection without skill is creating an argument.

5. *Use the "hum" technique.* This technique is a simplified version of asking questions that encourage the buyer of your services to open up (in sales, these are called *open-ended questions*). In addition, the hum technique couples asking open-ended questions with the "probe" sales skill. "Probing" means to ask more questions about a certain topic to get the inside story. Use this technique, introduced in week three.

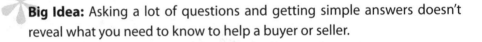

Big Idea: Asking a lot of questions and getting simple answers doesn't reveal what you need to know to help a buyer or seller.

6. *Tie down your benefit statement.* Sometimes agents get enamored with the sound of their own sales voices. The "tie-down" brings the buyer of your services back into the conversation, and allows you to check that you are still on track. This sales skill is introduced in week four. Use it throughout the sales cycle to ensure that the buyer of your services is still buying what you have to sell.

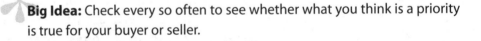

Big Idea: Check every so often to see whether what you think is a priority is true for your buyer or seller.

7. *Discover the motive that drives the buyers' decisions.* People make decisions based on feelings and rationalize these decisions with facts. However, few agents ever figure this out! They think people buy a particular home because it has three bedrooms! So they just keep showing three-bedroom homes in subdivisions until the buyer goes to another agent and buys a four-bedroom home on an acre—because it satisfies the buyer's emotional need for personal space.

But people don't share their dominant buying motives easily, especially when they don't know us. So, as salespeople, we are easily misled!

Let's say your friend buys a Mercedes. Does he say that he bought it because he wants status? No. He says he bought it because studies show the car will actually cost less in the long run because it will hold its value. While this may be true, your friend's desire for *status* (the emotional motivational driver) prompted his decision. Why else do you think people keep getting married for the fourth or fifth time? Because the facts tell them it's the right thing to do? Dream on!

This sales skill, discovering the buyer's driving motivator, is introduced in week four.

Big Idea: People make buying decisions based on emotions and rationalize them with the facts.

How These Sales Skills Work Together

As you can see from my explanations, each of these sales skills has a relationship to the other. That's why I picked this seven. That's why I want you to master each of them, so you become seamless in your sales communications with buyers of your services.

I Don't Want to Be Manipulative

I don't want you to be one of those manipulative salespeople, either! It would be manipulative if you used these skills with bad intent. But you are going to use these skills with good intent. That is, when you are asking questions and probing using the hum technique, you are going to find out whether it is in the best interest of the buyer to go ahead. You are going to tell him the truth attractively! Why? I want you to create a long-term referral/relationship business. The only way you will do that is to keep the customer's best interests in mind.

If you have good intent, the worst thing you can do is stop someone from making the buying decision he wants to make because you lack the sales skills to guide him through the process.

Big Idea: Keeping the customer's best interests in mind while you use sales communication skills ensures you do the right thing and build the right kind of business.

■ Sales Skill 1: Craft a Sales Call Script

The following method of crafting calls works for crafting any initial sales call. Because you needed this skill to start lead generating with your best source, people you know, you have already investigated it in context of that lead-generating source. Use the worksheet in Figure 10.1. It is very similar to the one in Section 8, which I've changed a bit here to be generic.

Here's the process:

1. Think of a particular person to call—or, of you're cold-calling, decide on the area you're calling and why
2. Determine potential real estate needs and benefits to this person that you can provide
3. Write three questions to ask this person to discover these needs
4. Determine your call objective
5. Write a question to get a lead or appointment—meet your objective
6. Write an opening statement

Example—Crafting a Cold Call

The *cold call* is a call you make to someone you know very little about. However, if you're calling a homeowner, you know the area in which the homeowner lives, and you can guess the homeowner may have one or more

---

FIGURE 10.1   Craft a Sales Call to Any Type of Contact

Name of person: _____

Potential real estate need(s): _____

Benefit to the person of your service: _____

Three questions:

    1. _____

    2. _____

    3. _____

Your call objective: _____

Question to get the order: _____

Opening statement: _____

Practice this sales call with a friend until you are comfortable.

of several common needs. Let's say you are making cold calls in an area of large homes. One need may be that the couple's children have grown, and they are looking to downsize.

Questions to ask:

1. Have you considered downsizing?
2. Do you know the value of your home?
3. Have you looked into freeing some of the equity in your home to purchase a rental home as an investment?

The call objective is to get an appointment. The question to get an appointment: When can we explore this potential? The opening statement is: I'm calling today to explore with homeowners in your area some possible real estate opportunities.

In Figure 10.2, I've written a possible script for you to use in a downsizing situation. Notice that I *start* with an attention-getting phrase. I *follow* with a statement that may be a need for them. I couple it with a statement about our company and mention that we work the area and have young buyers, so the seller knows I'm reputable. I *ask questions* to find out if they have a need. I follow the questions with a *close for an appointment,* adding *benefits* to the seller of that appointment.

Big Idea: The more focused the call on that particular potential client's needs, the more opportunity you will have of getting an appointment.

Immediately after the call, write a thank-you note and confirm your appointment. Put them in your database along with your appointment.

FIGURE 10.2 A Script for Cold-Calling

"Hello. This is Carla Cross with ABC Realty. I'll just take a minute of your time. I'm calling today to explore with homeowners in your area some possible real estate opportunities [*the attention-getting phrase*]. We specialize in your area, and we have young buyers with small children looking for homes there. Your area seems perfect for a young family, is that right? [*Yes.*] Have you thought of downsizing? [*Address their need.*] [*Yes.*] Do you know what your home is worth? [*No.*] In just a few minutes I can show you the market trends and how your home compares with what's selling today, so, if you do want to take an opportunity to downsize, you'll know the equity you have available [*feature and benefit to the seller.*]. I have some time Wednesday or Thursday evening. Would that work for you?" [*close*] Here's my name and phone number again, just for your records [*give them that information*]. Thank you. I look forward to meeting you."

Applying this Skill to Internet Situations

Let's say you get an Internet inquiry. As soon as possible, turn that cold inquiry into a warm relationship. Stop using e-mail to respond and pick up the phone. Craft a sales call to the inquirer, using the process I just outlined. The key here is to pick something the person asked you about that helps you get to know the person's lifestyle. For example, this particular inquirer is looking at homes with acreage. What do you need to know about his lifestyle that would start to form a relationship? After all, there are lots of reasons someone wants acreage. So, as you pick up the phone, one of your questions should be, "What will having acreage do for you?" Now you're starting to zero in on his lifestyle and his needs. To have a great call with this inquirer, you'll want to use the features/benefits, the hum technique, the tie down, and the ask a question to get the order sales skills. They all work together.

Big Idea: All these sales skills apply to every sales situation, proactive or reactive.

Practice, Practice, Practice

Have your friend or your manager give you a lead-generating situation (e.g., responding to an Internet lead). Create a sales call that helps you form a relationship, find out the needs, and close with a call to action. Role-play at least five different situations with your partner until you have mastered the process.

■ Sales Skill 2: Attach Benefits

A *benefit* is what a particular feature will do for the buyer of the feature. Example: this home has a fireplace. The fireplace is a feature, or fact. But what good is a fireplace if you don't need one for *something?* One benefit of a fireplace is that, when the electricity goes out, you can cook a meal in it! That may not be *your* primary benefit of having a fireplace in your home, but when our electricity was out for six days, it was a prioritized benefit to me! Buyers will be looking for the benefits of all the features you describe when you tell them about a particular property (see Figure 10.3).

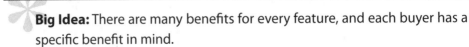

Big Idea: There are many benefits for every feature, and each buyer has a specific benefit in mind.

FIGURE 10.3 What's in It for Me?

The amateur salesperson's mistake. Too often a salesperson recites the facts (called *features* in sales) thinking that facts will sell the home. A great example of this is agents who answer floor inquiries. Wanting to provide all the information, they recite all the features of a home. Then, when the buyer hears a feature he doesn't want, he hangs up! Unless you attach a benefit to each feature, the buyer doesn't even know why something should be important to him! What is important and interesting to the buyer is *how he or she can use these features*. A three-car garage is a benefit to the person who owns three cars (or lots of things). It's merely an unwanted expense to a single person with one car!

Two ways to attach benefits. How do you discover what is important to a buyer?

1. One way is to ask a question about a feature. When a buyer requests a specific feature or need (e.g., a large family room), ask *why* or, a more graceful way to ask is, "What will having that do for you?" This tells you the benefit the buyer wants. Then, when you show a home with a large family room, remind the buyer that it provides plenty of space for that growing family. In this way, the buyer sees the relevance of the large family room.

Big Idea: Buyers make buying decisions based on the benefits of what that property will do for them.

2. Make a statement and attach a benefit. Then, ask if that's the benefit the person wanted. "This home has a *two-car garage* (feature), so that *you can park your two full-sized cars there* (benefit)." Benefits answer the buyer's question: so what? To attach benefits to features, state the feature first. Then, "bridge" to the benefit with the words "so that . . . "

Practice, Practice, Practice

Practice attaching benefits to the following features:

Feature	Bridge	Benefit
Family room . . .	so that	
Fireplace . . .	so that	
Low house payments . . .	so that	
Referrals to the agent are a benefit to the referring source because . . .		
Listing with me is a benefit to you, the seller, because . . .		
Working with me to find a home is a benefit to you, the buyer, because . . .		

Add benefits to features in at least 20 situations until adding benefits becomes second nature to you. This sales communication sounds so simple, but companies and salespeople constantly violate the rule (just read most recruiting brochures or real estate ads!).

Manager's Tip: Do a short training session during your sales meeting in which you first define features and benefits, give an example, and then let agents throw features at each other and attach benefits.

■ Sales Skill 3: Ask a Question to Get the Order

An "order" is a "yes" of any type. For example, you ask George if he wants to purchase that home. He says yes. You just asked for the order—and got an affirmative answer! Otherwise, you could be showing homes to George, find one he tells you he likes, and . . . nothing. George just doesn't know he's supposed to "turn himself in" and tell you he wants you to sell him that home. Most of the time, your buyer will not ask *you* to sell him a home! (That's not the buyer's job.) Our rule: to get an order, you must ask a question. Do buyers give salespeople a yes without being asked? Once in a while. But, if you're the salesperson, you shouldn't expect the buyer to take the sales pro's role, should you?

Big Idea: Successful salespeople always ask, but less successful salespeople are afraid to ask—and will miss golden opportunities to increase their businesses.

Practice, Practice, Practice

I know. This seems like such a simple skill, but about 50 percent of the agents who enter real estate sales each year are not "order askers." They have the habit of *not* asking for the order—in every part of their lives. If you're one of that 50 percent, you'll have to retrain your brain to ask for the order—if you want to make money in real estate.

To get in the habit, put 15 pennies in one pocket. Every time you ask for the order each day, put a penny in the other pocket. Get rid of all the pennies every day—for a month. Now, you have a new habit.

Also, when you're assigned this skill, ask a question to every person you talk to for a week. That will get you into the habit of asking questions.

Getting Leads When Knocking on Doors

When knocking on doors, you can phrase a question two ways:

1. *Direct question:* Are you thinking of selling/buying?
2. *Indirect question:* Do you know of anyone who is thinking of buying/selling?

■ Sales Skill 4: Use the AAA Method of Objection-Busting

An objection is a statement from a buyer that expresses his concern. It may be something like, "There is no formal dining room." Or, "I just want to wait until rates come down." Or, "I already have an agent." Just think of objections as one of the several "no's" that you need to accept from your buyer to get to "yes." Buyers give objections for lots of reasons:

1. They want to slow down the sales process because they're afraid to make a buying decision.
2. They have free-floating anxiety about making a buying decision, so they come up with reasons why they don't want to take a particular step forward.
3. They don't trust the salesperson.
4. They have a real concern.

Even though the first three reasons are smoke screens put up to take the salesperson off-course, even those must be handled with care to maintain a good relationship with the buyer.

Here's an easy way to learn how to handle objections, and it works. Use the method I created, which I call the "AAA" method:

1. Agree
2. Ask
3. Answer

When the objection comes from the buyer (the buyer of your services, whether a purchaser or seller), *agree* that she has an important point (the first A). You're not agreeing that the buyer is right. You're agreeing with her right to have a concern. After all, it's important to the buyer! Instead of telling her how she's wrong and jumping in with the right answer, slow down a minute. Execute the second A: *ask* more questions to discover just exactly what the buyer is talking about. Finally, after you've really probed as to the real concern, execute the third A: *answer* the objection with new information. Then, close!

The wrong way to handle objections. There's a wrong and a right way to handle those objections. Unfortunately, few real estate agents have been trained in answering objections effectively. Instead of focusing on the process, they focus on the answers. Their fear is that they won't have snappy answers to every objection. To lower their anxiety, they try to memorize all the answers—scripts they think will solve their problems. Armed with these scripts, they wait for an objection and pounce on the "right" answer! That just creates an adversarial relationship—and starts an argument!

The Script

The dialogue would go something like this:

Buyer: I want to wait to purchase. (objection)

You *agree:* I understand your concern. Buying is a big decision.

You *ask:* To help me understand exactly what you're thinking about, do you mind if I ask you a few questions?

You probe and ask more: Tell me more about waiting to purchase.

You provide an *answer:* There's some information that could help you make the best decision. Let me show you . . . Do you have any questions? Let's go ahead.

 Big Idea: Cushioning your answer with the first two As keeps the relationship intact.

Use the worksheet in Figure 10.4, Crafting an Objection-Buster, to create an objection-buster for each of the objections you are working on in *Up and Running.*

Using Visuals to Substantiate Your Objection Answers

We believe what we see, not what we hear. Yet, most of the time, agents fail to use visuals to substantiate the claims they make in answering objections. You can be much more credible if you use visuals—*evidence* that what you say is true. You have several assignments to create visuals to counter objections during your four-week *Up and Running* plan. It's not as difficult as you think. For instance, you know overpriced homes don't sell. But how can you prove it? There are several ways:

1. Show a comparison analysis. Find in your MLS figures for three-bedroom homes in a specific area that sold in the last 30 days. Find three-bedroom homes in that same price range and area that didn't sell. You will find that the sold homes were priced lower than the unsold ones.
2. As you inspect inventory, you will see a "right-priced" home that sells right away. You will also see a very similar home that is overpriced and doesn't sell. Take pictures of each, along with their MLS listing information, and put the two homes side by side in a comparison document. Show sellers that overpriced homes don't sell, while right-priced ones do.

FIGURE 10.4   Crafting an Objection-Buster

Objection

You **Agree** _____

You **Ask** _____

More Probing Questions

(Tell me more.) _____

(Please explain.) _____

(Then what happened?) _____

(How, what, when, why, how much?) _____

_____

You **Answer**

(Use visuals.) _____

_____

_____

_____

Close

_____

_____

_____

Excerpted from *Advantage 2.0,* Carla Cross Seminars, Inc.

The References Section Has Resources for You

See the References section for two more resources with processes, scripts, and role plays, plus two resources with dozens of ideas for substantiating your claims with visuals so you are believable. Also, see the National Association of REALTORS® studies, listed in the References section, which offer wonderful and credible statistics to use, including FSBO outcomes, market trends, and number of homes buyers viewed.

Manager's Tip: Purchase these NAR surveys every two years. Use them in your training to train your agents to "go visual" when countering buyer and seller objections.

■ Sales Skill 5: Use the "Hum" Technique

"I want a deal." Hearing that sentence strikes fear in the heart of a real estate agent! Why? Because we think we have to find the buy of the century. You assume you know what *deal* means to the buyer, and you show him homes that are overpriced by $20,000 so he can make an offer and get a "deal." Later, you find out that all he meant was that he wanted to pay $1,000 less than the list price! When we jump to conclusions about what someone means, we can go off in the wrong direction. "Deal" can mean many things: the best buy in the area, a fixer-upper, lots of money off the list price, special terms, and so on. To find out what the buyer means, we need a sales communication technique—the *hum technique*. This skill, a simplified version of the ask a question to get the order sales skill, is fun to use. It provides lots of information about what the buyer really wants and encourages the buyer to keep talking (while it forces you to keep listening!).

Big Idea: The person who listens best sells the most homes.

Here's the technique:

- Ask an open-ended question (one that requires more of an answer than yes or no). Hint: open-ended questions are those that start with who, what, when, where, how much, or why.
- Listen to the answer, pick out a core word, and repeat the word back to the talker, using a questioning upswing to your word. This will encourage your questioner to tell you more.
- As your talker talks, simply *hum*. This, too, will encourage the buyer to continue talking. You'll discover lots of information and show that you are a skilled, attentive listener.

There is a musical rhythm to the hum technique: core word as a question, followed by hums at appropriate places.

Big Idea: Open-ended questions start with who, what, when, where, how much, or why; they provide much more of an answer than just a yes or no.

The Script

Buyer: "I want a deal."

You: "Deal?" (Choose the main subject of the sentence and repeat it)

Buyer: "Yes. I want to buy at a fair price. I don't want to pay too much."

You: "Hmmmmmmm." This encourages the buyer to give you more information. Alternate saying key words with hums.

When to Use This Sales Skill

Use this skill all the time. Successful salespeople aren't good talkers; they're good listeners. See how long you can continue a conversation without actually saying a whole sentence. When you can talk with someone for three minutes and let him do all the talking, you're on your way to becoming an effective salesperson.

Practice, Practice, Practice

Practice this technique on your spouse or a friend for three days in a row. When you see this person in the evening, ask him how his day went. Listen. Pick on key words. Say them back, with a questioning tone. Keep him talking with a "hmmmmm." See how long you can sustain this dialogue (it's really more of a monologue) without saying a full sentence.

■ Sales Skill 6: Tie Down Your Benefit Statement

This is another simple sales skill, but one that's very important for creating rapport and agreement, and serves to move the sales process closer to a close. To use this technique, attach a question to your benefit statement. This cements the benefit in your customer's mind. Also, if you ask the buyer to agree with you on a particular benefit, and the buyer doesn't agree, you know he's after a different benefit for that feature. Now you know where to go in your sales communication.

Feature → *Benefit* → *Tie-Down*

The Script

Agent: "This home has a three-car garage (*feature*), which allows you to keep your antique cars at home so that (*bridge between feature and benefit*) you save rent (*benefit*). That is what you want, isn't it?" (*tie-down*)

Practice, Practice, Practice

Use Figure 10.5 to stay on track. Work in twos. One agent is the agent. The other agent is the buyer. Buyer: give a feature to your sales partner, the agent. ("I want a home with a large fenced yard.") Agent: state the feature,

FIGURE 10.5   Practice Tie-Downs

Feature	Bridge	Benefit	Tie-down question
Large lot Private setting Quiet street Low down payment	so that . . .	you can have . . .	That's what you want, isn't it?

attach a benefit with a bridge, and add a tie-down. ("This home has a large yard, so that your three children can play safely.") Do the exercise three times. Buyer: sometimes, agree with the tie-down. Sometimes, disagree, and let the agent change course. Now, reverse roles.

Manager's Tip: Use the above exercise as a training exercise in your new agent training or in your office meeting.

Big Idea: Tie-downs increase the motivation and clarity of purchase in the buyer.

■ Sales Skill 7: Discover the Motive That Drives the Buyers' Decisions

Of all the seven critical sales skills, I think this is the most important because using it ensures we can help a person make the right buying decision for him. What are motives? They are *emotional reasons* people take actions. People buy homes to *fill emotional needs*—motives. Homes with three bathrooms are not very motivating; however, providing personal space for your growing family is.

Big Idea: People make buying decisions to fill emotional needs.

Example: the buyer says, "I want six bedrooms." You ask, "Why?" Buyer answers, "To provide enough space so my five kids each have their own bedroom. I never had that growing up, and, as a kid, I vowed when I grew up, my family would have the privacy I wish I'd had." Wow—what a strong motivator to purchase the home he subjectively feels provides his family that personal space!

As a salesperson, you need to go way past the desired features and discover the *motives*. Develop an attitude like Detective Columbo. Always wearing an old raincoat, Columbo spent his time trying to discover people's motives for the crimes he investigated. Without identifying a motive, Columbo couldn't figure out who did it. But he was very clever to probe and probe until he found out who had the best motive, and he investigated until his suppositions proved him right. I'm going to show you how to investigate until you discover the motive, too.

Following the Evidence to Discover Dominant Buying Motives

In sales, we call these motives *dominant buying motives* (DBMs). They are the drivers that compel buyers to make buying decisions. These are the emotional needs the buyer is seeking to satisfy in every buying decision. We uncover a particular buyer's dominant buying motives by following the evidence. First, we gather the *features*. We do that every time we ask the buyer what he wants in a home. We ask the seller why he wants to sell, or where he's moving. These are the *facts*. (Most agents stop finding out what the buyer wants once he has gotten the facts. The agent runs out and shows homes to the buyer. He finds one he thinks the buyer should purchase. But the buyers won't make a buying decision. That's because facts aren't compelling. Emotions are. We'll take action to satisfy these strong emotional needs.)

Big Idea: Most buyers don't know their own dominant buying motives. Through expert questioning, we must help reveal them to the buyers, and remind the buyers of these DBMs when they find the home that would fulfill them.

Question more deeply. We need to question much more deeply than just asking for the facts. To get to the emotions, we attach benefits and check with the buyer or seller to see if those are the benefits she wants. Finally, we uncover the DBMs—those motives that are revealed by the benefits the buyer wants. We usually can't ask directly if the buyer wants to fulfill these needs. So, after we attach benefits, we need to listen for the strongest motive. Although buyers may want to fulfill several DBMs, there is always one that takes priority over the others. (Think of the buyer who wants a view home in a prestigious area, but gives it up when he finds there's no yard where his children can play. In this scenario, The DBM prestige fought with the DBM family security, and family security won!)

Big Idea: Facts aren't compelling. Emotional needs are.

Here are the main DBMs, and an example of each:

- *Personal space* (whatever a person feels gives him adequate personal space; this is not physical space, and could be 1,000 square feet for some and 10,000 square feet for others)
- *Prestige* (they want to live among famous people or in a prestigious area)
- *Security* (they want a gated community or a condominium with security)
- *Family security* (they want the best schools or a safe area for their children)

One motive always dominates the others. People often do not know their own dominant buying motives, but they can express their needs in terms of features. They can agree on benefits. You need to help them translate their physical needs to emotional needs.

Big Idea: People don't buy homes because it will be a "good investment." They're all good investments! What will the good investment do for you? Provide you *security*. There's the DBM.

Practice, Practice, Practice

Your exercise. Why did you buy your last home? Follow the evidence from the features to the benefits and uncover that DBM. You probably didn't know until you did this exercise!

Another exercise. Using Figure 10.6, pick three buyers you are working with or you just sold. What were their DBMs? If you don't have a clue, go back to the information you gathered when you interviewed them. Attach benefits. See which categories of DBMs the benefits fall into. Which

FIGURE 10.6   Dominant Buying Motives

Features They Want	Benefits to Them	Dominant Buying Motive

was their high priority? That is their DBM. Wouldn't it be a powerful, clarifying tool if you could help buyers uncover these DBMs?

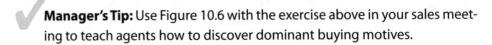

Manager's Tip: Use Figure 10.6 with the exercise above in your sales meeting to teach agents how to discover dominant buying motives.

Big Idea: In your interview process with buyers or sellers, make it a practice to uncover their DBMs. Arrange your questions so you start with features and then ask about benefits, so you can deduce their probable DBMs.

■ Summary

Mastering the seven critical sales skills is the "magic," the added ingredient you must develop to assure you get the biggest payoff from your lead-generating efforts. Developing these skills is the second most important thing you'll do. Of course, the most important thing you'll do is lead generate. Coupling your lead generation with your sales skills development gives you the most powerful one-two punch a new agent can have. So, get to work now in practicing these seven critical sales skills in your office—and in the field. You'll get much better payoffs, and a huge boost in your confidence level, too.

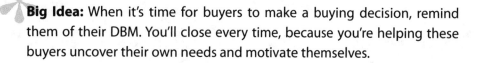

Big Idea: When it's time for buyers to make a buying decision, remind them of their DBM. You'll close every time, because you're helping these buyers uncover their own needs and motivate themselves.

The Completed *Up and Running* Start-Up Plan

Sample *Up and Running* Weekly Schedule for Week One

Week: One   Name: Joan Smith

Time	Monday	Tuesday	Wednesday	Thursday	Friday	Saturday	Sunday
7–8	Organize desk		Day off →	Write 40 follow-up cards			
8–9	Office meeting	Paperwork		→	Meet w/mgr	Paperwork	
9–10	Office tour	Call 20 people I know		Call 10 people to ask for leads	Call 20 people to ask for leads	Show homes	Show homes
10–11	→	→		→	→	→	→
11–12	Lunch	Floor time		Paperwork	Inspect	Lunch	Lunch
12–1	Office orient.	Lunch		Lunch	Lunch	Floor time	Follow-up
1–2	Inspect inventory	Start market analysis		Inspect inventory	Inspect	→	In-person visits to five people
2–3	→	→		→	Bus. support work	Inspect inventory	→
3–4	Call 20 people I know	Follow-up		Follow-up	→	Circle prospect 25 homes	
4–5	List 100 people to ask for leads	Inspect inventory		Meet with loan officer	Circle prospect 25 homes	→	
5–6	→	→		→	→		→
6–7							
7–8							Do listing presentation
8–9							→

Suggested Hours Weekly:

		What You Did
Lead generating	10	_____ hours
Qualifying buyers/sellers	5	_____ hours
Show properties/listing properties	5	_____ hours
Purchase/sale agreements	5	_____ hours

How could you improve your schedule?

Evaluate Your Weekly Schedule
Rate yourself in the effectiveness of your weekly schedule: _____
1–10 (10 is high)

Your *30 Days to Dollars* Lead-Generating Plan

Month: _____

Set your goals and track your results ("actuals")

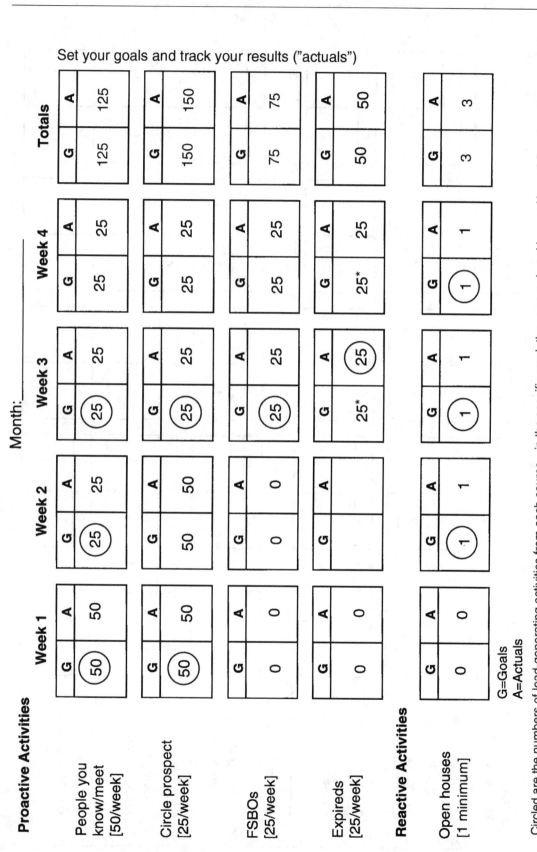

	Week 1 G	Week 1 A	Week 2 G	Week 2 A	Week 3 G	Week 3 A	Week 4 G	Week 4 A	Totals G	Totals A
Proactive Activities										
People you know/meet [50/week]	(50)	50	(25)	25	(25)	25	25	25	125	125
Circle prospect [25/week]	(50)	50	50	50	(25)	25	25	25	150	150
FSBOs [25/week]	0	0	0	0	(25)	25	25	25	75	75
Expireds [25/week]	0	0			25*	(25)	25*	25	50	50
Reactive Activities										
Open houses [1 minimum]	0	0	(1)	1	(1)	1	(1)	1	3	3

G=Goals
A=Actuals

Circled are the numbers of lead-generating activities from each source—in the specific week they are assigned in your *Up and Running* plan.

*By Week 3, you get to choose your favorite methods among those listed.

Your *30 Days to Dollars* Lead-Generating Results

Month: _____

Buyer Activities

	Week 1 G	Week 1 A	Week 2 G	Week 2 A	Week 3 G	Week 3 A	Week 4 G	Week 4 A	Totals G	Totals A
Qualifying interviews w/buyers	2	2	2	2	2	2	2	2	8	8
Qualified buyer showings	2	2	2	2	2	2	2	2	8	8
# sales							1	1	1	1

Listing Activities

	Week 1 G	Week 1 A	Week 2 G	Week 2 A	Week 3 G	Week 3 A	Week 4 G	Week 4 A	Totals G	Totals A
Qualified listing appointments	1	1	1	1	1	1	1	1	4	4
Marketable listings secured	0	0	0	0	0	0	1	1	1	1
# of listings sold	0	0	0	0	0	0	0	0	0	0*

G=Goals   A=Actuals

Note the results projected through time. These results are in your four-week *Up and Running* plan.

*Depends on your normal market time.

Yearly Goals and Monthly Activities

1. Set your monthly expections

Your $ expectations this year

$\boxed{\$ 72,000} \div 12 =$

Monthly expectation in $

$\boxed{\$ 6,000}$

2. Translate $ to revenue units*
   * "units" are numbers of sales and listings sold

Monthly expectation in $

Your $ earned sale per listing sold

Monthly unit goal

$\boxed{\$ 6,000} \div \boxed{\$ 6,000} =$ | 1/2 | 1/2 |

Listings sold   Sales

3. Plan activities to meet revenue unit goals using the numbers and ratios in *Up and Running*

	Month 1	2	3	4	5	6
Listings Sold	0	0	1	0	1	0
Listings Taken	1	0	1	0	0	1
Listing Appts.	4	4	4	4	4	4
Sales	1	1	0	1	0	1
Showing Appts.	8	8	8	8	8	8
Contacts (From *30 Days to $*)	400	300	200	200	200	200

The first month activities coincide with the *Up and Running* plan. Our agent follows the same contact plan she used for her third month onward to schedule her contacts and business results for the remainder of the year.

Sample Budget for the New Agent

Your Real Estate Budget
Real Estate Operating Expenses

Projections: 6 sales this year

                6 listings sold this year

                8 listings taken this year

	YEARLY	MONTHLY
Total marketing budget ($200 per listing/sale)	$2,800	$233
Professional fees (REALTORS, MLS)	600	50
Business car expenses (gas, oil, tools, repair)	2,400	200
Communication expenses (pager, phone)	1,200	100
Labor/mechanical	1,200	100
Professional development	600	50
Supplies	1,200	100
Business insurance	300	25
Legal fees / E&O	300	25
Licenses, permits	300	25
Other	1,200	100
TOTAL	$12,100	$1,008

Sample Budget Forecast

Month	1	2	3	4	5	6	7	8	9	10	11	12
Sales	1	1		1		1			1			1
Listings Sold			1		1		1		1		1	1
Income (closings)		6,000*	6,000	6,000	6,000	6,000	6,000	6,000	6,000	6,000	6,000	6,000
Expenses Out	1,008	1,008	1,008	1,008	1,008	1,008	1,008	1,008	1,008	1,008	1,008	1,008
Profit	(1,008)	4,992	4,992	4,992	4,992	4,992	4,992	4,992	4,992	4,992	4,992	4,992

Total income: $66,000
Total expenses: – $12,100
Profit: $53,900

*Note: If you make a sale in month one, that sale will be in month two, when the home closes. There is also a month lag from a sold listing to a closing.

Your Marketing Plan

1. Name your target market (who you're marketing to).
2. Put your actions in order of the dates to be accomplished.
3. Assign work to be accomplished in each tactic. Add your budget figure.
4. Tally your total budget from this target market.

Target Market: _____

Action	Assigned To	To Be Done By	Budget
Introduction	agent	1st month (Jan)	200 people @ 50 cents = $100
Phone calls (ask for referrals)	agent	2nd month (Feb)	200 people @ 25 cents = $50
e-Newsletter (one page)	agent	1st–2nd month (Feb)	200 people @ 25 cents = $50
"Spring Ahead" postcard	agent	3rd month (Mar)	200 people @ 30 cents = $60
Personal visit—seeds for spring plants	agent	4th month (April)	200 people @ 50 cents = $100
e-Newsletter (one page)	agent	5th month (May)	200 people @ 25 cents = $50
"Just Listed" postcard	agent	6th month (June)	200 people @ 30 cents = $60
Phone calls (ask for referrals)	agent	7th month (July)	200 people @ 25 cents = $50
e-Newsletter (one page)	agent	8th month (Aug)	200 people @ 25 cents = $50
"Just Sold" postcard	agent	9th month (Sept)	200 people @ 30 cents = $60
Personal visit—pumpkins	agent	10th month (Oct)	200 people @ $1 = $200
e-Newsletter (one page)	agent	11th month (Nov)	200 people @ 25 cents = $50
Holiday card	agent	12th month (Dec)	200 people @ 50 cents = $100

Notes:
E-Newsletter 4 times/year; preprinted postcards 3 times/year
Regularly send anniversary cards to each person you sold
Take housewarming gift within 2 weeks after closing (to both buyers and sellers)
Increase your postcards (just listed/just sold) as you can, to prove you are a successful agent

Blank Forms for Your *Up and Running* Plan

These forms will be used either at the beginning of your program or throughout your four weeks.

■ Part One

To Complete as You Begin Your Program:

- Agreement to Ensure You're *Up and Running*
- Get Ready: Gather the Tools of the Trade
- Yearly Goals and Monthly Activities
- Budget for the New Agent
- Budget Forecast
- Your Marketing Plan
- Portfolio Exercise
- Technology Budget and Planner

To Complete Each Week:

- Your *30 Days to Dollars* Lead-Generating Plan (spreadsheet)
- Your *30 Days to Dollars* Lead-Generating Results (spreadsheet)
- Tracking Qualified Buyers
- Buyer's Potential Evaluator
- Listing Presentation Qualifier
- Marketable Listing Evaluator

Agreement to Ensure You're *Up and Running*

I, _____, agree to complete all the assignments in the *Up and Running in 30 Days* start-up plan. I understand each aspect of the plan, and that it is constructed to help me get a fast start.

I want support from my manager, so I agree to make an appointment with my manager weekly. During that appointment, I will review the work completed for that week and my plan for the next week. I agree to:

1. Keep each appointment

2. Be on time

3. Be prepared

To ensure that I get the most from my plan, I expect my manager to:

- Meet with me weekly for at least one-half hour

- Help me keep my activities prioritized correctly

- Provide assistance in my development of specific business methods

- Provide me any resources necessary to complete the assignments

- Provide the support and encouragement necessary to begin a successful career

I understand it's my business, and I agree to manage it according to the principles in *Up and Running in 30 Days*.

Agent _____   Manager _____

Date of this agreement: _____   End of program: _____

Get Ready: Gather the Tools of the Trade

Briefcase

Cell phone

Pen

Pencil

Colored pen or pencil

Calendar

Highlighter

Scratch pad

Post-it notes

Daily planner or PDA

Access to your MLS

Street map

Paper clips

Tape measure (100' or 30.5m)

Staple gun

Laptop computer

Hand-held calculator

Digital camera

Attitude notebook*

Office notebook*

Resource notebook*

Car

Sold signs

Tape

Mallet and nails

Screwdriver

Flashlight

Coveralls

Overshoes

First aid kit

Forms

Purchase and sale agreements

Wording for contract forms

Other contract addendas

Listing agreements

Other forms pertaining to listing

Other Materials

_____

_____

_____

*See "Get Ready—Get Organized"

Yearly Goals and Monthly Activities

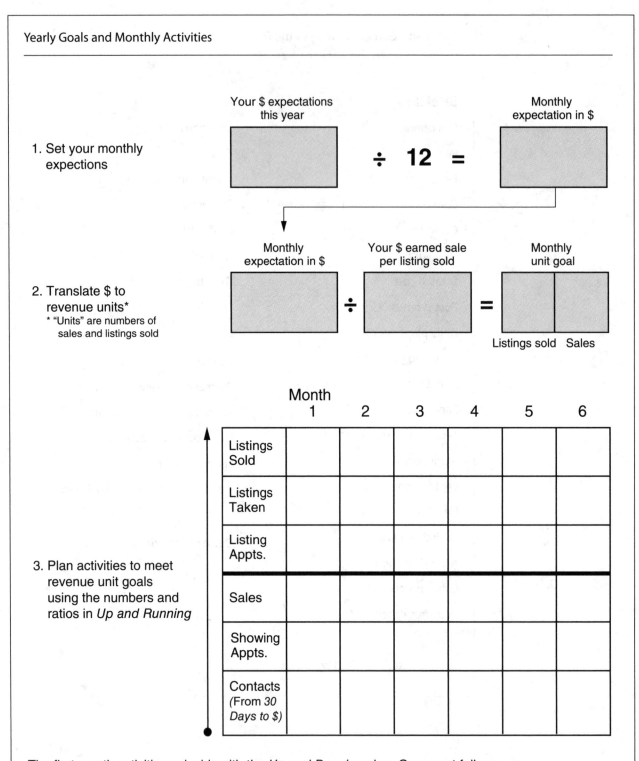

1. Set your monthly expections

Your $ expectations this year

÷ **12** =

Monthly expectation in $

2. Translate $ to revenue units*
   * "Units" are numbers of sales and listings sold

Monthly expectation in $

÷

Your $ earned sale per listing sold

=

Monthly unit goal

Listings sold   Sales

3. Plan activities to meet revenue unit goals using the numbers and ratios in *Up and Running*

Month	1	2	3	4	5	6
Listings Sold						
Listings Taken						
Listing Appts.						
Sales						
Showing Appts.						
Contacts (From *30 Days to $*)						

The first month activities coincide with the *Up and Running* plan. Our agent follows the same contact plan she used for her third month onward to schedule her contacts and business results for the remainder of the year.

Budget for the New Agent

Your Real Estate Budget
Real Estate Operating Expenses

Projections: _____ sales this year

                     _____ listings sold this year

                     _____ listings taken this year

	YEARLY	MONTHLY
Total marketing budget ($200 per listing/sale)		
Professional fees (Realtors, MLS)		
Business car expenses (gas, oil, tools, repair)		
Communication expenses (pager, phone)		
Labor/mechanical		
Professional development		
Supplies		
Business insurance		
Legal fees / E&O		
Licenses, permits		
Other		
TOTAL		

Budget Forecast

Month	1	2	3	4	5	6	7	8	9	10	11	12
Sales												
Listings Sold												

Income												
Out												
Net												

Net Profit:

Your Marketing Plan

1. Name your target market (who you're marketing to).
2. Put your actions in order of the dates to be accomplished.
3. Assign work to be accomplished in each tactic. Add your budget figure.
4. Tally your total budget from this target market.

Target Market: _____

Action	Assigned To	To Be Done By	Budget
Introduction			
Phone calls (ask for referrals)			
e-Newsletter (one page)			
"Spring Ahead" postcard			
Personal visit—seeds for spring plants			
e-Newsletter (one page)			
"Just Listed" postcard			
Phone calls (ask for referrals)			
e-Newsletter (one page)			
"Just Sold" postcard			
Personal visit—pumpkins			
e-Newsletter (one page)			
Holiday card			

Notes:

E-Newsletter 4 times/year; preprinted postcards 3 times/year
Regularly send anniversary cards to each person you sold
Take housewarming gift within 2 weeks after closing (to both buyers and sellers)
Increase your postcards (just listed/just sold) as you can, to prove you are a successful agent

Portfolio Exercise

List Your Skills	Benefits to Buyers/Sellers	Show It—Evidence

Technology Budget and Planner

Use this planner to create an action plan to purchase and implement the technology you feel will support your career best during your first few months in the business. Put a date to acquire each item. Put a price beside each item, so you'll have a technology budget. Add up your costs so you can allocate a portion of your funds each month to technology. Check off as you achieve your technology goals.

	Priority	Date to Acquire	Cost	Achieved
A laptop computer, so you can work from anywhere				
Database for your prospects, clients, and affiliates				
Contact management program to run your marketing plan				
Capture and follow up on your Internet leads				
Measure your progress toward your goals software/service				
Cell phone to keep in contact with your customers				
PDA or smart phone				
Personal Web page				
Digital camera				
Financial management software				

Your *30 Days to Dollars* Lead-Generating Plan

Month: _____

Proactive Activities	Week 1		Week 2		Week 3		Week 4		Totals	
	G	A	G	A	G	A	G	A	G	A
People you know/meet [50/week]	◯		◯		◯		◯			
Circle prospect [25/week]	◯		◯		◯		◯			
FSBOs [25/week]					◯		◯			
Expireds [25/week]					◯					
Reactive Activities										
Open houses [1 minimum]			◯		◯		◯			

G=Goals
A=Actuals

Proactive means you go out and find a prospect.
Reactive means you wait for a prospect to come to you.

Circled are the numbers of lead-generating activities from each source—in the specific week they are assigned in your *Up and Running* plan.

Your *30 Days to Dollars* Lead-Generating Results

Month: _____

Buyer Activities

	Week 1		Week 2		Week 3		Week 4		Totals	
	G	A	G	A	G	A	G	A	G	A
Qualifying interviews w/buyers	◯		◯		◯		◯			
Qualified buyer showings	◯		◯		◯		◯			
# sales							◯			

Listing Activities

	Week 1		Week 2		Week 3		Week 4		Totals	
	G	A	G	A	G	A	G	A	G	A
Qualified listing appointments	◯		◯		◯		◯			
Marketable listings secured					◯					
# of listings sold										

G=Goals   A=Actuals

Tracking Qualified Buyers

Record and qualify your buyer leads

Date of Qualifying Meeting	Name	Address	Questionnaire Used?	Both @ Qualifying Session?	# Showings	Sales

Buyer's Potential Evaluator

Rate on a scale of 1–4 (4 is the highest)

1. Buyer answered all qualifying questions.	1 2 3 4
2. Buyer is motivated to purchase. (Rate each spouse/partner separately.)	1 2 3 4
3. Buyer is realistic about price range expectations.	1 2 3 4
4. Buyer is open and cooperative.	1 2 3 4
5. Buyer will purchase in a timely manner.	1 2 3 4
6. Buyer is a referral source and will provide referrals.	1 2 3 4
7. Buyer has agreed that you will be his or her exclusive agent.	1 2 3 4
8. Agent has established a positive rapport with buyer.	1 2 3 4
9. Buyer will meet with loan officer.	1 2 3 4
10. Buyer answered financial questions openly.	1 2 3 4
11. Buyer has no other agent obligations.	1 2 3 4
12. If buyer has home to sell, he or she is realistic about price.	1 2 3 4
13. Buyer will devote sufficient time to purchasing process.	1 2 3 4
14. Both spouses/partners will be available to look for home.	1 2 3 4
15. This buyer is worthy of my time, energy, and expertise.	1 2 3 4

Use this evaluator with each buyer to ensure you are working within your standards to achieve effective time management and referrals.

Listing Presentation Qualifier

Date of Presentation	Name	Address	Want to Sell?	Both Home?	2 Hours Pre-Scheduled?	How Much $ Want?	Marketing Presentation Completed?	Results

Marketable Listing Evaluator
_____

1. Property listed at competitive price   Yes_____   No_____

2. Full-term listing agreement   Yes_____   No_____

3. Seller to complete obvious repairs/cleaning prior to showing   Yes_____   No_____

4. Easy access (e.g., key, phone for showing)   Yes_____   No_____

5. Yard sign   Yes_____   No_____

6. Immediate possession   Yes_____   No_____

7. Extras included (e.g., appliances)   Yes_____   No_____

8. Available for first tour   Yes_____   No_____

9. FHA/VA terms available   Yes_____   No_____

10. Owner financing available   Yes_____   No_____

11. Below market down payment   Yes_____   No_____

12. Below market interest rate   Yes_____   No_____

13. Post-dated price reduction   Yes_____   No_____

14. Market commission   Yes_____   No_____

15. In my evaluation, this property will sell within listed market range,
    in normal market time for this area.   Yes_____   No_____

16. I will receive referrals from the sellers.   Yes_____   No_____

Use this evaluator with each of your potential listings to ensure sellers meet your standards.

■ Part Two

Planning and Tracking Documents for Each of the Four Weeks of *Up and Running*

> ### W E E K   O N E

- Your Weekly Schedule for Week One
- Your Daily Planner
  (This is your "master." Make one copy per day for this week.)
- Your Start-Up Plan and Accomplishments for Week One

Up and Running Weekly Schedule for Week One

Week: _____

Name: _____

Time	Monday	Tuesday	Wednesday	Thursday	Friday	Saturday	Sunday
7–8							
8–9							
9–10							
10–11							
11–12							
12–1							
1–2							
2–3							
3–4							
4–5							
5–6							
6–7							
7–8							
8–9							

Suggested Hours Weekly:

		What You Did
Lead generating	10	_____ hours
Qualifying buyers/sellers	5	_____ hours
Show properties/listing properties	5	_____ hours
Purchase/sale agreements	5	_____ hours

How could you improve your schedule?

Evaluate Your
Weekly Schedule
Rate yourself in the
effectiveness of your
weekly schedule: _____
1–10 (10 is high)

Daily Planner

_____

Date: _____

Priorities:	Accomplished	Notes:

Priorities: **Accomplished**   **Notes:**

1. _____ ❏ _____

2. _____ ❏ _____

3. _____ ❏ _____

4. _____ ❏ _____

5. _____ ❏ _____

6. _____ ❏ _____

7. _____ ❏ _____

8. _____ ❏ _____

9. _____ ❏ _____

10. _____ ❏ _____

	Lead Generating	Qualified Leads	Listing Appointments	Home Showings
Activity				
Hours Spent				

	Listings Obtained	Sales	Listings Sold
Results			

Rate your efforts on a scale of 1–10 _____

How can you improve your rating? _____

_____

Make six copies of this form each week.

Your Start-Up Plan and Accomplishments for Week One

Check Off When Completed   Manager's Comments

Business Producing

Implement Your *30 Days to Dollars* Lead-Generating Plan

❑ Contact at least 100 people using these methods:

    ❑ Call or contact 50 people you know (see Section 8 for a script)

    ❑ Circle prospect 50 people (see Section 8 for definition and operation)

    ❑ Other: _____

❑ Get two qualified seller leads

❑ Get two qualified buyer leads

❑ Show homes to two qualified buyer groups

❑ Go to at least one listing appointment

Business Supporting

Regular weekly/daily actions:

❑ Create your weekly schedule in advance of the following week

❑ Create your daily schedules each day using daily planner

❑ Add at least 50 contacts to your database

❑ Write at least 15 follow-up notes

❑ Evaluate your buyers and sellers using the buyers and sellers evaluation sheets

❑ Do the activities in your marketing plan

❑ Do the activities in your technology plan

❑ Practice the sales skills assigned in this week

❑ Apply the sales skills that are assigned for this week in real life

❑ Add to your resource notebook

❑ Add to your attitude notebook

❑ Add to your office notebook

Measure Your Results

❑ Daily planner—evaluate your actions each day

❑ Weekly schedule—evaluate at end of week

❑ Weekly accomplishments—check off actions

❑ Goals/actuals spreadsheets—compare your results with the *Up and Running* plan

Additional Business-Supporting Activities for Week One

Sales skills

❑ Using sales skill #1, craft a sales script to call on people you know (see Section 8)

❑ Using sales skill #3, ask for a lead (see Section 10)

❑ Create three visuals to counter seller's objections to pricing

Your Start-Up Plan and Accomplishments for Week One (continued)

Check Off When Completed   Manager's Comments

Sales opportunities

❑ If you're going to hold open house or take floor time: get information from your manager on how to do each of these reactive lead-generating activities.

❑ Observe two public open houses this weekend. Interview the agents who holds them open about their methods.

❑ Observe at least one hour of floor time this week (or, if you don't have floor time, observe three agents handling incoming calls).

❑ Interview the agent who takes floor time about their methods.

Technical information

❑ Orientation: Complete all your office orientation duties (get your business cards, etc.). Put all the information in your office notebook.

❑ Meet with a loan officer to learn the basics of financing (get a loan officer referral from your manager). Put all that information in your resource notebook.

❑ Ask three experienced agents to see their market analyses packages. Take notes so you can compile your own. Then, complete a market analysis on your own home. Practice presenting it to a "seller," so you'll be comfortable with the format and information.

Planning

❑ Use the Your Real Estate Budget form to complete your budget

❑ Use the Technology Planner to make your technology plan

❑ Use the Marketing Plan Planner to create your marketing plan (see Section 9 for how to create your plan and for a sample plan)

WEEK TWO

- Your Weekly Schedule for Week Two
- Your Daily Planner
- Your Start-Up Plan and Accomplishments for Week Two

Up and Running Weekly Schedule for Week Two

Week: _____   Name: _____

Time	Monday	Tuesday	Wednesday	Thursday	Friday	Saturday	Sunday
7–8							
8–9							
9–10							
10–11							
11–12							
12–1							
1–2							
2–3							
3–4							
4–5							
5–6							
6–7							
7–8							
8–9							

Suggested Hours Weekly:

		What You Did
Lead generating	10	_____ hours
Qualifying buyers/sellers	5	_____ hours
Show properties/listing properties	5	_____ hours
Purchase/sale agreements	5	_____ hours

How could you improve your schedule?

Evaluate Your Weekly Schedule
Rate yourself in the effectiveness of your weekly schedule: _____
1–10 (10 is high)

Daily Planner

_____

Date: _____

Priorities:	Accomplished	Notes:
1. _____	❏	_____
2. _____	❏	_____
3. _____	❏	_____
4. _____	❏	_____
5. _____	❏	_____
6. _____	❏	_____
7. _____	❏	_____
8. _____	❏	_____
9. _____	❏	_____
10. _____	❏	_____

	Lead Generating	Qualified Leads	Listing Appointments	Home Showings
Activity				
Hours Spent				

	Listings Obtained	Sales	Listings Sold
Results			

Rate your efforts on a scale of 1–10 _____

How can you improve your rating? _____

_____

Make six copies of this form each week.

Your Start-Up Plan and Accomplishments for Week Two

Check Off When Completed   Manager's Comments

Business Producing

30 Days to Dollars Lead-Generating Plan

❏ Contact at least 100 people using these methods:

  ❏ Call or contact 25 people you know (see Section 8 for a script)

  ❏ Circle prospect 50 people (see Section 8 for definition and operation)

  ❏ Call on at least 25 for sale by owners or expired listings (see Sections 8 and 9 for skill development)

  ❏ Hold one open house

❏ Get two qualified seller leads

❏ Get two qualified buyer leads

❏ Show homes to two qualified buyer groups

❏ Go to at least one listing appointment

Transfer these numbers to your goals/actuals spreadsheets for week two so you can track your progress through time.

Business Supporting

Regular weekly/daily actions:

❏ Create your weekly schedule in advance of the following week

❏ Create your daily schedules each day using the daily planner

❏ Add at least 50 contacts to your database

❏ Write at least 15 follow-up notes

❏ Evaluate your buyers and sellers using the buyers and sellers evaluation sheets in Section 12

❏ Do the activities in your marketing plan for that second week

❏ Do the activities in your technology plan

❏ Practice the sales skills assigned for this week

❏ Apply the sales skills that are assigned for this week in real life

❏ Add to your resource notebook

❏ Add to your attitude notebook

❏ Add to your office notebook

Measure Your Results

❏ Daily planner—evaluate your actions each day

❏ Weekly schedule—evaluate at end of week

❏ Weekly accomplishments—check off actions

❏ Goals/actuals spreadsheets—compare your results with the *Up and Running* plan

Your Start-Up Plan and Accomplishments for Week Two (continued)

Check Off When Completed   Manager's Comments

Additional Business-Supporting Activities for Week Two

Practice new sales skills

❑ Sales skill #4: Objection-Busting (refer to Section 10 for more information)

❑ Apply the sales skills that are assigned for this week in real life

❑ Assemble listing presentation materials

❑ Interview three agents in your office about listing presentations

❑ Interview three agents in your office about three common objections and how they handle them

❑ Assemble buyer presentation materials

❑ Interview three agents in your office about buyer presentations

❑ Interview three agents in your office about three common buyer objections and how they handle them

❑ Write two purchase and sale agreements

WEEK THREE

- Your Weekly Schedule for Week Three
- Your Daily Planner
- Your Start-Up Plan and Accomplishments for Week Three

Up and Running Weekly Schedule for Week Three

Week: _____   Name: _____

Time	Monday	Tuesday	Wednesday	Thursday	Friday	Saturday	Sunday
7–8							
8–9							
9–10							
10–11							
11–12							
12–1							
1–2							
2–3							
3–4							
4–5							
5–6							
6–7							
7–8							
8–9							

Suggested Hours Weekly:

		What You Did
Lead generating	10	_____ hours
Qualifying buyers/sellers	5	_____ hours
Show properties/listing properties	5	_____ hours
Purchase/sale agreements	5	_____ hours

How could you improve your schedule?

Evaluate Your Weekly Schedule
Rate yourself in the effectiveness of your weekly schedule: _____
1–10 (10 is high)

Daily Planner

_____

Date: _____

Priorities:	**Accomplished**	**Notes:**
1. _____	❏	_____
2. _____	❏	_____
3. _____	❏	_____
4. _____	❏	_____
5. _____	❏	_____
6. _____	❏	_____
7. _____	❏	_____
8. _____	❏	_____
9. _____	❏	_____
10. _____	❏	_____

	Lead Generating	Qualified Leads	Listing Appointments	Home Showings
Activity				
Hours Spent				

	Listings Obtained	Sales	Listings Sold
Results			

Rate your efforts on a scale of 1–10 _____

How can you improve your rating? _____

_____

Make six copies of this form each week.

Your Start-Up Plan and Accomplishments for Week Three

Check Off When Completed   Manager's Comments

Business Producing

30 Days to Dollars Lead-Generating Plan

❑ Make 100 sales calls:

    ❑ 25 to people you know

    ❑ Circle prospect 25

    ❑ Choose from other methods for another 50 proactive contacts

    ❑ What you chose: _____

    ❑ Hold one open house

❑ Secure two qualified buyer appointments

❑ Show homes to two qualified buyer groups

❑ Secure one appointment to do a listing presentation

Caveat: If you are not getting enough appointments, increase your lead generating.

Transfer these numbers to your goals/actuals spreadsheets for week three so you can track your progress through time.

Business Supporting

Regular weekly/daily actions:

❑ Create your weekly schedule in advance of the following week

❑ Create your daily schedules each day using the daily planner

❑ Add at least 50 contacts to your database

❑ Write at least 15 follow-up notes

❑ Evaluate your buyers and sellers using the buyers and sellers evaluation sheets

❑ Do the activities in your marketing plan for that second week

❑ Do the activities in your technology plan

❑ Practice the sales skills assigned for this week

❑ Apply the sales skills that are assigned for this week in real life

❑ Add to your resource notebook

❑ Add to your attitude notebook

❑ Add to your office notebook

Measure Your Results

❑ Daily planner—evaluate your actions each day

❑ Weekly schedule—evaluate at end of week

❑ Weekly accomplishments—check off actions

❑ Goals/actuals spreadsheets—compare your results with the *Up and Running* plan

Your Start-Up Plan and Accomplishments for Week Three (continued)

Check Off When Completed   Manager's Comments

Additional Business-Supporting Activities for Week Three

❑ Apply sales skill #5, the "hum" technique (see Section 10)

❑ Gain performance excellence with sales skill #5 (see Section 10)

❑ Create ten reasons why people should choose you

❑ Write two purchase and sale agreements

❑ Practice your listing presentation three times (see your manager for a presentation or see the References section)

❑ Practice your buyer presentation three times (see your manager for a presentation or see the References section)

❑ Gather three visuals to counter seller's objections (see your manager or the References section)

❑ Gather three visuals to counter buyer's objections (see your manager or the References section)

WEEK FOUR

- Your Weekly Schedule for Week Four
- Your Daily Planner
- Your Start-Up Plan and Accomplishments for Week Four

Up and Running Weekly Schedule for Week Four

Week: _____   Name: _____

Time	Monday	Tuesday	Wednesday	Thursday	Friday	Saturday	Sunday
7–8							
8–9							
9–10							
10–11							
11–12							
12–1							
1–2							
2–3							
3–4							
4–5							
5–6							
6–7							
7–8							
8–9							

Suggested Hours Weekly:

		What You Did
Lead generating	10	_____ hours
Qualifying buyers/sellers	5	_____ hours
Show properties/listing properties	5	_____ hours
Purchase/sale agreements	5	_____ hours

How could you improve your schedule?

Evaluate Your Weekly Schedule
Rate yourself in the effectiveness of your weekly schedule: _____
1–10 (10 is high)

Daily Planner

Date: _____

Priorities:	**Accomplished**	**Notes:**
1. _____	❑	_____
2. _____	❑	_____
3. _____	❑	_____
4. _____	❑	_____
5. _____	❑	_____
6. _____	❑	_____
7. _____	❑	_____
8. _____	❑	_____
9. _____	❑	_____
10. _____	❑	_____

	Lead Generating	Qualified Leads	Listing Appointments	Home Showings
Activity				
Hours Spent				

	Listings Obtained	Sales	Listings Sold
Results			

Rate your efforts on a scale of 1–10 _____

How can you improve your rating? _____

_____

Make six copies of this form each week.

Your Start-Up Plan and Accomplishments for Week Four

Check Off When Completed   Manager's Comments

Business Producing

30 Days to Dollars Lead-Generating Plan

❏ Make 100 sales calls: you choose type

   ❏ What you chose: _____

❏ Hold one open house

❏ Secure two qualified buyer appointments

❏ Show homes to two qualified buyer groups

❏ Secure one appointment to do a listing presentation

❏ List one marketable property

❏ Sell one home

Caveat: If you are not getting enough appointments, increase your lead generating.

Transfer these numbers to your goals/actuals spreadsheets for week four so you can track your progress through time.

Business Supporting

Regular weekly/daily actions:

❏ Create your weekly schedule in advance of the following week

❏ Create your daily schedules each day using your daily planner

❏ Add at least 50 contacts to your database

❏ Write at least 15 follow-up notes

❏ Evaluate your buyers and sellers using the buyers and sellers evaluation sheets

❏ Do the activities in your marketing plan

❏ Do the activities in your technology plan

❏ Practice the sales skills assigned in that particular week

❏ Apply the sales skills that are assigned for this week in real life

❏ Add to your resource notebook

❏ Add to your attitude notebook

❏ Add to your office notebook

Measure Your Results

❏ Daily planner—evaluate your actions each day

❏ Weekly schedule—evaluate at end of week

❏ Weekly accomplishments—check off actions

❏ Goals/actuals spreadsheets—compare your results with the *Up and Running* plan

Your Start-Up Plan and Accomplishments for Week Four (continued)

Check Off When Completed   Manager's Comments

Additional Business-Supporting Activities for Week Four

❑ Practice and apply sales skills #6 and #7 (see Section 10)

❑ Complete the entire listing process materials, including a market analysis package

❑ Review and complete your qualifying/interview package for buyers

❑ Complete your personal promotional materials—a professional portfolio and/or your personal brochure

❑ Gain performance excellence in two new sales skills (you choose from the seven critical sales skills)

❑ Add three more visuals to counter objections sellers give you (to your seller presentation)

❑ Add three more visuals to counter objections buyers give you (put in your buyer presentation)

Sample Scripts and Letters

■ A Script for Calling on People You Know

"Hi, Sally. I have been thinking about you. I'm in real estate now. Oh, you got my announcement postcard? Good. I've already learned to stay in contact frequently, since I guess agents aren't the best with that! Yes, I'm with ABC Realty, a wonderful firm in downtown Bellevue. Oh, you know that firm? Yes, I think I made a great decision. I wanted to call and let you know I'm working hard to do things right. I just got through my training school, and, boy, is there a lot to learn! It was great, though, and I feel really prepared to help people now. Yes, I have two sales and three listings so far. Yes, that's really great for a new agent! Also, I work with George Snell, who is my manager and coach. So, for these first few months, I have a real expert looking over my shoulder every step, which, I think, helps my clients feel comfortable. It's kind of a "two for one" benefit. Do you know anyone who needs my help? Great. [*Take down the information. Ask who, when, where, can you use Sally's name.*] Well, thanks again and I'll talk with you soon."

Immediately after the call,

1. send that handwritten note of thanks for the lead, and
2. put that information in your database.

■ A Script for Cold-Calling

"Hello. This is Carla Cross with ABC Realty. I'll just take a minute of your time. I'm calling today to explore with homeowners in your area some possible real estate opportunities [*the attention-getting phrase*]. We specialize in your area, and we have young buyers with small children looking for homes there. Your area seems perfect for a young family, is that right? [*Yes.*] Have you thought of downsizing? [*Address their need.*] [*Yes.*] Do you know what your home is worth? [*No.*] In just a few minutes I can show you the market trends and how your homes compare with what's selling today, so if you do want to take an opportunity to downsize, you'll know the equity you have available [*feature and benefit to the seller*]. I have some time Wednesday or Thursday evening. Would that work for you?" [*Close*] Here's my name and phone number again, just for your records. [*Give them that information.*] Thank you. I look forward to meeting you."

Immediately after the call,

1. write a thank-you note and confirm your appointment, and
2. update your database along with your appointment.

■ A Script for Converting the FSBO

First visit: "Hi. I'm Carla Cross with ABC Realty. I noticed your sign just went up. Selling your home? Great. I'd like to give you some information to help you. Why? We need "sold" signs in the neighborhood to show buyers it's a very desirable place to live. Here's [*name the piece of information you're handing them*]. I know it will be useful to you because it [*fill in the benefits, using sales skill #2, explained in Section 10*]. I'll check in next week to see how it's going. Thanks for your time."

Second week and subsequent weeks: "Hi, Carla Cross again with ABC Realty. How's it going? [*Seller will probably tell you it's going great.*] Good. Was the information helpful that I dropped off last week? [*Seller probably won't remember what it was, but will tell you it was helpful.*] Great. Here's another item that I've found really helpful to sellers. [*Give them the item.*] I'll check back with you later."

Around week five: "Hi, this is Carla (oh, you remember …). How's it going? Is there anything about the information I've given you that I can help you with? Questions? [*Seller will, at this point, be getting desperate. He will use your question as a rationalization to invite you further.*] Okay. I'd love to answer that, but now is not a good time. I could come over tonight or tomorrow night. Which would be better for you? [*If the individual has a partner ask what time works for both—you want both parties there.*]

At the presentation: First, answer their questions. Then, go into your presentation. "I appreciate your time. Here's the answer … Let me show you how I work, so you'll have the benefit of choosing the right person should you decide to list your property." [*Now, do your listing presentation.*]

■ The Expired Listing Script

Opening: "Hello. I'm Carla Cross of ABC Realty. Is your home still on the market? [*They may have re-listed and it isn't in your MLS yet.*] [*If no …*] Are you still interested in selling at some point? [*If yes, or maybe, or sometimes, even no*] I'll tell you why I ask. I work in this area, and would like to stay abreast of the properties available. In case I get a buyer for your home, I'd like to be prepared so your property is represented properly. Do you have about three minutes? [*If yes, go ahead. If no, ask*] What time would be convenient for me to give you a call?

Survey questions: What do you feel are the biggest selling points of your home? That sounds like it should be attractive to many buyers! What kind of buyer do you feel would be attracted to your home? Why? Why do you feel it didn't sell? What do you feel was the best marketing the agent did? What would you have liked to see? If you were to list again, what would you be looking for in a listing agent? When and where are you moving? [*Use the "feel" words. Don't criticize the other agent. Just get the information and hum in agreement.*] [*If you don't have an opportunity to ask these questions, or you feel it isn't appropriate to ask all the questions on the phone, save them to ask at the appointment. You need to qualify this seller!*]

Close: It sounds as though you have a very sellable property if just a few adjustments are made. I'd love the opportunity to share my thoughts with you. [*If you have a successful track record, tell the seller now.*] I'm proud to say that I've helped [*or, our office has helped*] many sellers get their homes sold after they'd been unsuccessful with a different agent. Could I come over at [*time*] or [*alternate time*] when both of you would be home? It would take no more than 45 minutes, and you could tell me "not interested" at any time! If you decide not to sell your home at this time, at least you will have a different perspective. And, hopefully you'll think of me if you decide to sell in the future."

Immediately after the call: Optimize your impression. Send a thank-you note within one day of your call or visit.

■ The Circle Prospecting Script

"Hi. I'm Carla Cross with ABC Realty. We just listed the Smith home down the street. Have you seen the property? No? I'm going to be holding it open this weekend, and I'd love to invite you over. I'll even have coffee and cookies. I'm sure you'll be interested to see how the Smiths have creatively remodeled that trilevel. The listing price is $347,500. Here's a flyer with all the information and the open house date and time. By the way, [*ask an indirect or direct question to get a lead*]:

Indirect: Do you know anyone in the area who has thought of selling?

Direct: I see your home is one of the largest in the area. Have you thought about downsizing?

Thanks for your time. I'll check back, because I'll be letting you know when the property sells."

Immediately after the call: Optimize your opportunity. Write a thank-you note within one day of your meeting, thanking them for their time and enclosing your card.

■ Script: Quick Qualifying Questionnaire for Buyers

- How long have you been looking for a home?
- What attracted you to this home?
- When do you want/need to move?
- Have you been prequalified by a lender?
- Are you working with a real estate agent?

■ Quick Seller Qualifier

- When do you want/need to move?
- Where are you moving?
- Have you ever sold a home before?
- What are you looking for in a listing agent?
- When can I come over and preview the home and visit with you?

■ Letter: Introduction to Your Career in Real Estate to People You Know

Dear _____,

I'm writing you this note to let you know I've just begun a new career. I'm now selling real estate with _____ [*insert your company name*]. It's an exciting profession, and I've already found that my background in _____ [*fill in your pertinent background*] has helped prepare me well for my new profession. In addition, I've had the benefit of attending a wonderful training program at our company, and I'm being coached by _____ [*put in your manager or coach's name*] so I'm getting the guidance and advice agents need to really be of service to buyers and sellers.

With all this knowledge and training behind me, I'm excited to help buyers and sellers. If you know of someone who wants to buy or sell in our area, please let me know. I'll give them the very best service I can, backed by the great reputation of my company, and the support of my manager.

If I can answer questions about the state of the market for you, I'd love to do that, too. I'm keeping abreast of the market trends and prices in your area.

My contact information:

Your name
Office name
Office address

Phone
Fax
E-mail

Sincerely,

[your name]

To optimize this, write a short, handwritten note at the bottom of each of your letters.

■ Internet Reply Note

Dear _____,

Thank you for inquiring about homes in our area. I have lived here for 15 years and love it, and would welcome an opportunity to show you why when you visit. It looks to me as though you need four bedrooms. Do you have children? Or, do you need a space for an office? If you'll let me know your needs for bedrooms/offices, and so on, I'll help you narrow your scope to preview the right properties for you. I know it can be overwhelming to see all those properties without some filters.

My contact information:

Your name
Office name
Office address

Phone
Fax
E-mail

Sincerely,

[*your name*]

References

Here are training, marketing, and systems references for you to use as you start your business.

■ Training Resources

These sales and management resources are available from Carla Cross Seminars, Inc. and Carla Cross Coaching at *www.carlacross.com.* Quality tested: more of Carla's resources have been reviewed and are recommended by the Real Estate Brokerage Managers' Council (CRB) and the Council of Residential Specialists (CRS), the two highest designations available to real estate professionals, than any other training provider.

Career Achievement Coaching

From Carla Cross Coaching, your next step after *Up and Running:* one-on-one coaching with a real estate–specific coach trained by Carla Cross. This is for real estate agents looking to take their careers to the next level; it builds further than the principles of *Up and Running.* Schedule: once a week for the first month (45 minutes), then twice a month for the next five months (30-minute calls). This program includes a client manual, two complimentary CDs, a 20-page behavioral profile interpretation, *The Business Planning System for the Real Estate Professional,* and three other professional systems (over $800 of professional systems included).

Companions to This *Up and Running* Resource

Up and Running in 30 Days companion CDs, a four-CD set, is not available in bookstores. It includes the following:

- Three audio training CDs, a complete tutorial from Carla covering the important concepts of the program, and additional sales tips to implement the program. This is a "behind the scenes" look at this quick-start program; it includes what it takes to succeed, motivates new agents, and provides additional training support to managers implementing the program.

- Role plays: The audio CDs include actual role plays of the critical sales skills scripts and lead-generating scripts introduced in the book for additional training tools.

- Additional processes and systems on the document CD: letters, scripts, forms, and an Excel spreadsheet to measure progress, plus four bonus forms not in the book.

Quality tested and recommended by the Real Estate Brokerage Managers' Council (CRB).

BIG IDEAS: What I Wish I'd Known When I Started Selling Real Estate!

A compilation of the words of advice in *Up and Running*, plus more tips for success and plenty of motivation and inspiration.

To Market Yourself

Your Professional Portfolio, Carla Cross Seminars, Inc., 3rd edition 2007. How to market yourself to get client loyalty and highest commissions. Raises confidence and increases competitive advantage. 100 pages, 1 audio CD, plus 1 document CD, with 11 bonus forms.

◼ In-Depth Resources to Train and Coach Your Agents

1. *Up and Running* Team Coaching

Carla Cross's trained, professional coaches coach and train new agents with the *Up and Running* principles. Teleconference plus audio, hard-document training tools. Special company pricing. Three months, weekly, 45 minutes. Includes a 250-page training/coaching handbook with intensive, specific guidance, *Up and Running in 30 Days* book and four-CD set, personalized DISC behavioral profile report (20 pages), and three complete professional systems (*The Complete Buyer's Agent Toolkit, Your Client-Based Marketing System*, and *Your Professional Portfolio*—over $800 worth of systems included in this program to train your agents so you don't have to.) Goal: get new agents a sale fast.

2. *Advantage 2.0* Training in a Box

Up and Running on steroids! High-accountability in-office training/coaching program for new agents. Eight sessions over two months. In the starter kit:

- Five student guides, complete with audio CDs and a systems/forms CD
- One facilitator guide, with CDs—how to teach effectively for best results—the newest teaching methods
- Administrator toolkit, with all the accountability forms you'll need on CD
- PowerPoint presentation on CD, to present professionally and easily

Use this program after you've had your agents start their businesses with the *Up and Running* start-up plan so you have them running from the first day in the business and you get results much faster. See *www.carlacross.com* for more information on systematizing your training with the New Agent Development System (NADS), which shows you how to coordinate *Up and Running* and Advantage 2.0 to get best results.

Quality tested and recommended by the Real Estate Brokerage Managers' Council (CRB).

For Long-Term, Detailed Business Planning

The Business Planning System for the Real Estate Professional. Carla Cross Seminars, 2nd edition 2007. Training and all the forms to write an effective business plan—a complete tutorial. A 170-page manual with all business-planning forms. Includes two audio CDs and bonus document CD with ready-to-use forms, including four Excel interactive spreadsheets to track and record goals. The most-used business planning system in the world by real estate professionals and people in leadership positions.

Quality tested and recommended by the Council of Residential Specialists (CRS).

For Prospective Agents and Those New to Real Estate

Become Tomorrow's Mega Agent Today! Carla Cross, Noteworthy Publishing, 2004. Use this book to get the rest of the information you need to start your career right. A 240-page book with budgets, time lines, and job descriptions for new agents. Makes a great recruiting tool for managers, too. Includes new agent expectations survey and real estate trends, plus 77 interview questions new agents should ask—and managers should be prepared for.

Recommended by CRB and CRS.

To Create an Effective Sellers' Process— The Complete System

Your Client-Based Marketing System, Carla Cross, Carla Cross Seminars, Inc. A complete tutorial on working with sellers, plus all the forms and presentations an agent needs; covers from the first phone call to after closing. 280 pages with 35 checklists, processes, and systems. 20 visuals to anticipate and counter objections. Gain loyalty, confidence, and get SOLD listings. PowerPoint presentation, two audio CDs with role plays and how-tos, many forms on included forms CD for your customization.

Quality tested and recommended by CRS.

To Create an Effective Buyer's Process—The Complete System

Your Complete Buyer's Agent Toolkit, Carla Cross Seminars, Inc. A complete tutorial, along with all the systems and forms for a buyer's agent. An agent's guide to selling more buyers faster and creating lifelong loyalty. Inside the Toolkit, three buyers packages: *The Pre-Appointment Package, Your Guide to Purchasing a Home,* and the *Home Buyer's System.* Over 235 pages of detailed information along with over 25 checklists and processes to manage the buying process. This is truly an at-home study program for professional buyer agency.

Quality tested and recommended by CRS.

Objection Busters

Never be stumped by an objection again! Learn how to "bust" any objection with Carla's AAA method. The method is carefully spelled out, so you can apply it to any objection. You'll be in control of all situations! Colorful flash cards help you learn fast and easily. Hear role plays of the most common objections. Most common objections are role-played on the accompanying CD.

- *Buyer Series (Objections Buyers Give):* 8 common objections and 16 answers; role-play dialogue and written scripts
- *Seller Series (Objections Sellers Give):* 6 common objections and 18 answers; role-play dialogue and written scripts
- *Recruiting Series (Objections Recruits Give):* 6 common objections and 14 answers; role-play dialogue and written scripts

■ Marketing Resources

Carla Cross Seminars, Inc. does not recommend or endorse the following resources. These are listed solely for your convenience, and do not represent all the resources available in any given area. These resources supply materials for your marketing plan. Some of them also offer Web site design and/or lead-generation management.

Prospects Plus	800-287-5710	*www.prospectsplus.com*
The Personal Marketing Company	800-458-8245	*www.tpmco.com*
QuantumMail	800-637-7373	*www.quantummail.com*
Sendsations	800-800-8197	*www.sendsations.com*
Virtual Agent Office	877-422-2826	*www.virtualagentoffice.com*

Internet Lead Generation and Management; Web Design

Most Home Technologies	*www.mosthome.com*
Katabat Corporation	*www.katabat.com*
House Values	*www.housevalues.com*
Wolfnet Technologies	*www.wolfnettech.com*
Favorite Agent	*www.favoriteagent.com*
Virtual Agent Office	*www.virtualagentoffice.com*

For Real Estate Statistics to Use in Presentations

National Association of REALTORS® Profile of Home Buyers and Sellers: *www.realtor.org/research*. These reports are published every two years from extensive surveys of buyers and sellers done by your National REALTOR® organization. These reports are a treasure trove of buyer/seller habits, and should be used in your presentations to prove what you know to be true.

Software For Financial Management

Quicken	*www.quicken.com*
Quickbooks	*www.quickbooks.com*
Money	*www.microsoft.com/money*

Software for Contact Management

Top Producer	*www.topproducer.com*
Outlook	*www.microsoft.com/outlook*
Carla Cross Coaching: Business and Client Management	*www.carlacrosscoaching.com*

Software for Accountability/Business Plan Measurement

Carla Cross Coaching: Business and Client Management	*www.carlacrosscoaching.com*

INDEX

A

Accountability, xxviii–xxix, 11, 42–43, 53
Accountability software, 227
Acknowledgment, 66
Action, 95–96
Action plan, 70
Activities
    concentration on, 50–51
    monthly, 45
Activity plan, 19
Adaptability, 28–29
Adjustments, 39
Advantage 2.0, 225
Agent choice, 29
Agreement to Ensure You're Up and Running, 60–61, 182
Area selection, 121
Ask for a lead, 122
Attaching Benefits to Features, 163
Attitude, 64–68, 71
    managing shifts, 65–66
    notebook, 66–67, 75, 77
    recognition, 66

B

Bank of America Homeowners Services, 115
Become Tomorrow's Mega Agent Today!, xv, 44, 225
Beethoven, 12
Behavioral profile, 26–27
Believable conclusion, 68
Benefits
    attachment, 153, 158–60
    tie-down, 154, 166–67
Best sources, 113–14
Brain retraining, 67–68
Breakeven, 50
Brochure, 108, 124, 149
Budget, 177, 185
    creation, 47, 48–49
    forecast, 178, 186
Bush, President, 28
Business cycle, 21, 52

Business path, 20–22, 52
Business plan measurement, 227
Business Planning System for the Real Estate Professional, The, 223, 225
Business producing, xxvi–xxvii, 22–23
    week one, 73, 74, 76–77
    week two, 88
    week three, 100, 105
    week four, 107–8, 109–10
Business producing, xxvi–xxvii
Business sources, 33
Business supporting, xxvi–xxvii, 23, 57–58
    assignment, 75
    week one, 73, 77–78
    week two, 88
    week three, 100–101, 105
    week four, 108–9
Buyer
    activities, 41
    consultative session, 134
    evaluation sheet, 77
    presentation, 90–91
Buyer qualification, 131, 132, 134–37
    script, 218
    tracking, 192
Buyer's Potential Evaluator, 57, 136, 137, 193

C

California Association of REAL-TORS®, 9, 29
Calling people known script, 215
Career goals, 4–5
Carla Cross Coaching, 221
Carla Cross Seminars, Inc., 39, 222–24
CD package, 39, 223–24
Cell phone, 8
Certified Real Estate Broker (CRB), xxv
Circle prospecting, 26, 34–35, 74, 120–22, 123
Circle prospecting script, 220

Closing, 132
Coaching, xxviii–xxix, 2, 13–14, 17, 59–60, 62–63, 71
Cold calling, 26, 27,156–57, 218
Commissions, shrinking, 2, 14–15, 18
Communicator, long-term, 29–30
Comparison analysis, 163
Complete Buyer's Agent Toolkit, The, 224
Complete Recruiter, The, 138
Comprehensive client question-naire, 139
Conative Connection, The, 95
Conclusions, 65
Confidence, 83
Consistency, 123, 143
Consultative meeting, 139, 141
Contact(s), 39, 116
    database, 77
    information, 31
    number of, 33, 38
    skills, 58
Contact management program/software, 8, 225
Conversion ratios, 42–43
Conversions, 125
Craft a sales call, 122
Crafting an Objection-Buster, 163, 164

D

Database, 8, 32
Daily Planner, 77, 79, 89
    creation of, 81–83
    week one, 198,
    week two, 203
    week three, 208
    week four, 213
Decision making
    motivation, 154–55, 167–70
    time, 29
Definitions, 76
Demanding attention, 60–61
Dependent tendencies, 63–64
Desk fee, 3
Developable salesperson, 12